DiVine MAKEOVER

God Makes You *Beautiful*

By Sharla Fritz

CONCORDIA PUBLISHING HOUSE · SAINT LOUIS

This study is dedicated to
the awesome young women of Trinity Lutheran Church in Lisle, Illinois,
who helped with the creation of this book. Your faith, commitment,
and generosity inspire me.
You truly "Shine" with God's love and grace.

Published by Concordia Publishing House

3558 S. Jefferson Avenue, St. Louis, MO 63118-3968

1-800-325-3040 · www.cph.org

Copyright © 2014 by Sharla Fritz

Manufactured in the United States of America

1 2 3 4 5 6 7 8 9 10   23 22 21 20 19 18 17 16 15 14

Table of Contents

Introduction 5

Week One

Step into a Divine Makeover and Fashion
Your Life for True Beauty................................... 8

Fashion Finesse: Modesty Myths and Truths.................. 34

Week Two

Hang Up the Uniform and Let Go of Your
Inner Control Freak... 38

Fashion Finesse: The Power of Fashion............................ 61

Week Three

Bag the Handbag of Worry and Carry
an Attitude of Trust.. 63

Fashion Finesse: Beautiful Bags 87

Week Four

Pitch the Prom Dress of Pride and Wear
Humility Instead 90

Fashion Finesse: Seven Tips for a
Fabulous Formal.. 115

Week Five

Get Rid of Envy Green and Put On the Color
of Contentment.. 116

Fashion Finesse: Color Yourself
Confident... 143

Week Six

Boot Out the Boots of Selfishness and Step Out in Shoes of Love...146

Fashion Finesse: A Pair of Shoes.........................171

Week Seven

Unravel the Bitterness Sweater and Choose to Wear Forgiveness..173

Fashion Finesse: The Shape of Sweaters.............199

Week Eight

Look in the Mirror and See a New You.................200

Fashion Finesse: Faith and Fashion— Putting It All Together..227

Extras

Brand-New Clothes...229

What If I Don't Have Good Parents?....................230

Setting Boundaries...233

Study Guide Answers..234

Endnotes..239

Introduction

Imagine. Cameras flash. Applause fills the room. Faces light up as you step through the door. Cries of "You look amazing!" reach your ears.

Your friends rush in to hug you, careful not to mess up your hair or wrinkle your designer clothes. They gasp at the four-inch platforms on your feet and squeal over the French manicure on your hands.

You have just participated in a fashion makeover. You look beautiful. And for the moment, you feel like a celebrity.

* * * * * * *

Would you love the chance to be on a makeover show? Would you like to remake your look? As a young woman, maybe you struggle with feeling good about yourself. Maybe it seems you don't measure up to the world's standard of beauty.

Divine Makeover: God Makes You Beautiful will lead you through a makeover of the heart. As you journey through these pages, God will restyle your spirit, so that, even on the days you're not happy with what you see in the mirror, you can discover your true beauty in God's love for you. This makeover will alter your soul and change you from the inside out.

There really is a makeover show in the Bible. Ephesians 5:25–27 tells us that Jesus' mission was to clean up every spot and blemish He sees in the Church—and in all of us—and transforms us into an image of perfection and holiness! We are able to walk that runway because Jesus loves us enough to wash our souls with His amazing forgiveness and give us the ultimate makeover.

Each week this Bible study will focus on a character quality, an inner beauty, that we receive from Him. The week is divided into five daily readings with study guides—forty days in all.

Each day's reading takes just a few minutes, but you can spend as much time as you like to work through the study guide. Each week of the study includes a few questions designed to be discussed in a group. That way, if you're part of a Bible study group (or if you'd like to start one!), you can experience the divine makeover together.

Whether you use this Bible study with a group or on your own, I hope that this format will help you get into a daily routine of meeting with your Savior. I encourage you to mark up your book. Underline or highlight passages that inspire or challenge you. Make notes. Ask questions.

There are a few tools that are used often in this book:

Get a close-up. Zoom in on one thing you discovered today. I ask this question every day because I want you to pick out one thing that made you think "Wow! I didn't know that," or "Mmm . . . I never thought about that before." Write down one truth that will make a difference in your everyday life.

Memory verse. Each day you will be asked to write out the memory verse for the week. The act of writing out the words will help you to store the verse in your mind. You might also want to write out the Scripture on a sticky note that you post on your mirror or in your locker or carry in your backpack as a way to remind you of God's truth for you.

Study Styles. Every week, the Study Styles section will teach you a new way to study God's Word. These sections take a little longer to finish, but I hope that learning new ways to look at the Bible will help you dig deeper into the Word of God and its truth for you. Once you have learned these new study styles, you might want to use them with other Bible passages.

Meaningful Makeover. The Bible is full of fascinating people and amazing stories, but if all we get out of it is learning some new facts, we have missed the point. God transforms us through His Word. The weekly Meaningful Makeover section helps you learn how to apply God's Word to everyday life and experience that makeover for yourself.

Fashion Finesse. Although the focus of this book is inner beauty, I have included a little fashion fun. Each week, I conclude with a few words about finding the right clothes, building a wardrobe, and looking your best.

As a young woman, you are still discovering your own style. You're probably experimenting with clothes, hairstyles, and makeup to find your best look. And it's easy to get caught up in the world's manic obsession with physical beauty.

My prayer is that this book will help you focus on inner beauty. I pray that you will discover a joy that outshines any lip gloss. May you find your loveliness, not in trendy makeup or the latest fashions, but in God's awesome love for you!

Maybe you won't be on a television makeover show. Maybe cameras won't follow your transformation. Applause won't fill the room. But God's divine makeover will transform your heart, soul, and mind. In His grace, your beauty will shine!

WEEK ONE

Step into a Divine Makeover and Fashion Your Life for True Beauty

Memory Verse

> Put off your old self, which belongs to your former manner of life and is corrupt through deceitful desires . . . [and] put on the new self, created after the likeness of God in true righteousness and holiness.
>
> Ephesians 4:22, 24

Day One

◇◇◇◇◇◇◇◇◇◇◇◇◇◇◇◇◇◇◇◇◇◇◇◇◇◇◇

A Fashion Makeover

Put off your old self, which belongs to your former manner
of life and is corrupt through deceitful desires . . . [and]
put on the new self, created after the likeness of God in
true righteousness and holiness. Ephesians 4:22, 24

It took only two episodes, and I was hooked.

I first watched the show *What Not to Wear* during a weekend spent visiting relatives. For two days, my sister-in-law and her two teenage daughters tuned in often to the *What Not to Wear* marathon on television. They were already big fans of the fashion makeover program, and it didn't take long for me to discover why.

I admit it. It was kind of fun to laugh at the participants who were spotted wearing ratty old sweat suits. It was a blast to watch all mouths in the room drop open at the sight of the tacky and shocking outfits some of the women wore.

Best of all, it was incredible to see how these women were totally transformed. Stacy and Clinton, the hosts of the show, helped each woman find just the right clothes for her shape. Hair stylists and makeup artists brought out her best features. By the end of the show, the lady in the ratty sweat suit with the messy ponytail was almost unrecognizable as she stepped out in a gorgeous new outfit and perfectly styled hair. She looked amazing.

If you had seen me in my younger years, you definitely would have started a campaign to get me on the show. You would have called Stacy and Clinton and demanded that they devote two full episodes to make over this wardrobe-challenged girl. Someone should have told me not to wear the pink dress printed with daisies the size of Frisbees. And the pair of purple corduroy (gasp!) flares. And especially the raspberry-red plaid coat that was four sizes too big.

I struggled in the fashion department when I was in high school. I envied the girls who seemed to have it all together. The ones whose outfits always coordinated perfectly. The ones with cover-girl beauty who looked amazing in everything they wore.

Meanwhile, I kept wearing the wrong thing; I continued to make horrible clothing choices. I could have used a wardrobe consultant, a style expert, or just a friend who wasn't afraid to tell me the awful truth and help me choose a better wardrobe.

What about you? Maybe your clothes aren't as bad as mine were, but would you jump at the chance for a fashion makeover?

We don't all have the chance to be on a makeover show, but we all have a Spiritual Fashion Advisor. We each have the opportunity to learn from the Expert on how to fashion our lives for real beauty.

God is our Makeover Expert. Now, He isn't all that concerned about what is appearing on New York fashion runways. And although He certainly wants us to dress modestly, I doubt that He cares if we wear pleated pants instead of skinny jeans. He doesn't give us fashion demerits if we buy our sweaters at Walmart instead of dELiA*s.

But while God probably doesn't tune in to TV makeover shows, He does watch how we clothe our character. In Christ, He loves us just as we are, and, in Christ, He makes us much more. The Holy Spirit gives us a divine makeover. Through God's Word, He transforms our hearts. Through Christ's body and blood in the Lord's Supper, He alters our souls.

In the Bible, God encourages me to take off the old self (Ephesians 4:22). My old self is wrapped up in selfishness and envy. It's the part of me that gets hopeless and desperate to impress, that keeps wearing doubt and fear, worry and guilt. It's the part of me that will do anything necessary to impress my friends.

When I want to dress for success, my old self does its best to dress me in the lies and ugliness of sin. Sure, I want to be prettier and smarter. I want to be more successful and more popular. Who doesn't? Yet even while I'm struggling for all of those things, the lie that those things will make me happy keeps me in the rags of worry and shame.

Our heavenly Makeover Artist keeps telling me, telling you, "Girl, you don't have to keep wearing those old rags. I have something better for you."

The clothes God gives make us pure in His sight (v. 24). Through faith in Jesus' death and resurrection, we are forgiven. We are made completely new.

So step into this makeover and watch the Holy Spirit work. He can throw off your fear and cover you in hope. He can fling off your worry and wrap you in peace. He'll toss out your shame and clothe you in love.

It's time for a new design. Will you trust the Holy Spirit to work a miraculous transformation in your heart?

I nominate you for a divine makeover. May the Holy Spirit work through this Bible study to clothe you with His own impeccable and perfect design!

Dear Father in heaven, I thank You that You love me, even seeing my flaws! Help me to trust You as You work a divine makeover in my life. Help me to be willing to throw out the old clothing that wraps me with lies. Give me peace and grace as Your Son makes me shine. In Jesus' name. Amen.

Looking Your Best

Any style consultant worth paying for would do one thing: bring out your best qualities!

What do you like about yourself? Your picture-perfect skin? Long legs? Charming smile? Great hair? Choose makeup and fashions that play up your loveliest features.

Day One
◇◇◇◇◇◇◇◇◇◇◇◇◇◇◇◇◇◇◇◇◇◇◇◇◇
Wardrobe Workout

1. Imagine that a famous style consultant is coming to look in your closet. What wouldn't you want her to see? Pull it out and ask yourself why you keep it. If you are doing this study in a small group, bring this item to the meeting and discuss why we hold onto things we really should get rid of.

2. Read Ephesians 4:22–32.

   a. The apostle Paul, the author of Ephesians, tells us to "put off" certain behaviors and to "put on" others. Why do you think he used this picture of putting off and putting on?

   b. Verse 22 instructs us: "Put off your old self, which belongs to your former manner of life and is corrupt through deceitful desires." The world is full of deceitful desires—things that promise to make us happy, but then fail to deliver that happiness. Below are listed a few of these "deceitful" desires in our reading today. List any others you can think of.

   • desire for beauty

   • desire for intelligence

   • desire for success

   • desire for popularity

   _____

   _____

   _____

   _____

   _____

   _____

c. Verse 24 says that our new self is created to be like God! Jesus—the perfect likeness of God—makes our new self possible. What are some qualities of God that you would like to see more of in your life?

3. Get a close-up. Zoom in on one thing you discovered today. What did God teach you that will make a difference in your life?

4. Our memory verse for this week is Ephesians 4:22, 24: "Put off your old self, which belongs to your former manner of life and is corrupt through deceitful desires . . . [and] put on the new self, created after the likeness of God in true righteousness and holiness." To help you memorize this passage, make it your screen saver on your phone or computer this week. Also write it out in the space below—the simple act of typing or writing the words will make them stick in your brain.

Day Two

Crucial Clothing

I will greatly rejoice in the LORD; my soul shall exult in my
God, for He has clothed me with the garments of salvation;
He has covered me with the robe of righteousness.
Isaiah 61:10

"Look at this," my husband said, handing me the newspaper. "Stacy London is coming to the mall this Saturday."

"Really? Stacy London? Coming to our mall?!"

I could hardly believe it. The article in the paper said that the popular host of *What Not to Wear* was coming to *my* town to kick off the fall fashion season.

Saturday morning, I hunted through my closet for my cutest outfit (I didn't want Stacy to sign me up for her show on the spot) and headed for the mall. Once there, I discovered that after I had a meet and greet with the television host, her fashion team would give me some wardrobe advice.

How cool was that?

So after I had my picture taken with Stacy (woohoo!), I met with one of her assistants—a real-life New York fashion consultant. She began by asking me a few questions: What were my fashion essentials? What did my wardrobe need?

Putting together a cute wardrobe that you will actually wear means buying clothes that are not only stylish, but that fit your lifestyle. If you love to buy party dresses but never have any parties to wear them to, you're wasting your money. I have to ask myself, what kind of clothes do I need?

When it comes to spiritual fashion, we don't have to wonder what is most essential. The Bible tells us what we really need to clothe our souls:

> I will greatly rejoice in the LORD; my soul shall exult in
> my God, for He has clothed me with the garments of
> salvation; He has covered me with the robe of righteousness.
> Isaiah 61:10

The most important pieces in our spiritual closet are the "garments of salvation" and the "robe of righteousness." These are the "party dresses" we need to get into the biggest celebration ever—heaven.

"Okay," you say. "I hear you. We need garments of salvation and robes of righteousness. But what *is* righteousness anyway? What do garments of salvation look like? Why would I even want to wear them?"

Being righteous essentially means being declared "not guilty." We've all messed up. We've told little white lies or big black lies. We've gossiped to our friends or screamed at our parents. We've snubbed the unpopular girls or ignored the kids who don't quite fit in. And all our sins show up as big black stains on our hearts.

But you know what? Jesus loves us anyway. He sees the dirt on our souls, but He says, "Don't worry. I've taken care of it; I've washed you clean. Here, let Me take that filthy thing you're wearing. I have a beautiful robe for you instead."

The robe of righteousness is what allows us to stand before God without shame. It's what enables us to know Jesus as a loving friend instead of a harsh judge.

But of course, we can't get that robe on our own. We can't buy it at Target or at the designer outlet mall. No amount of money can buy this important garment. In fact, if God were running an advertising campaign, it might go something like this: "Fashion T-shirt: $20. The latest jeans: $45. Robe of righteousness: priceless."

Jesus Himself had to buy that robe for us with His own blood. Now God gives it to us—for free—when we receive the gift of faith in Christ, our Savior, through the Word. He brings us through the waters of Baptism and transforms our spirits. The Father holds out the robe of righteousness and invites us to slip our arms into the sleeves. He wraps us in the garments of salvation and clothes our hearts with His Spirit and His love. (If you are not sure you have received these garments, please check out page 229.)

I had fun that Saturday at the mall when the New York fashion consultant helped me find just the right clothes for my everyday life. But even better, God gives all of us the clothes we need for eternal life.

Let's remember to thank God for cleansing our grimy spirits and giving us clean hearts.

Almighty God, thank You for giving me salvation; I know there is nothing I could do to earn it on my own. Jesus, thank You for paying the price for my sin through Your death and resurrection. Holy Spirit, thank You for clothing me in righteousness. Amen.

Finding Your Fashion Essentials

To determine your own fashion must-haves, make a list of activities you participate in regularly, the kinds of clothing you need for them, and the number of items you need to get you through to laundry day. What do you need for

• school? _____

_____

• church? _____

_____

• work? _____

_____

• sports? _____

_____

• special occasions? _____

_____

After you have made your list, check your wardrobe to see if you have everything necessary.

Day Two
◇◇◇◇◇◇◇◇◇◇◇◇◇◇◇◇◇◇◇◇◇◇◇◇
Wardrobe Workout

1. What clothes in your closet do you consider essential? Why are they your go-to garments?

2. We talked a lot about the robe of righteousness today. Using what you learned today, write your own definition of *righteousness*.

3. Read Zechariah 3:1–5. In this passage, Zechariah tells about a vision he had of a priest named Joshua who gets a divine makeover.

   a. Imagine yourself in Joshua's place, with Satan pointing his finger at you, ready to accuse you of everything you have done wrong. What feelings do you experience?

   b. This passage is full of symbolism. What do you think the "filthy garments" (v. 4) picture?

c. What do the "pure vestments" (v. 4) or "fine garments" (NIV) symbolize?

d. Who takes off Joshua's filthy garments and puts on his clean robes? What do you think this means?

4. Get a close-up. Zoom in on one thing you discovered today.

5. Write out our memory verse for this week: "Put off your old self, which belongs to your former manner of life and is corrupt through deceitful desires . . . [and] put on the new self, created after the likeness of God in true righteousness and holiness" (Ephesians 4:22, 24). Read a phrase, then cover it and write it. Try to write as much of the verse as you can without looking.

Day Three
◇◇◇◇◇◇◇◇◇◇◇◇◇◇◇◇◇◇
Unfading Beauty

*Do not let your adorning be external—the braiding of
hair and the putting on of gold jewelry, or the clothing
you wear—but let your adorning be the hidden person
of the heart with the imperishable beauty of a gentle and
quiet spirit, which in God's sight is very precious.
1 Peter 3:3–4*

"Hey, Mom, can I buy this mascara?"

"Can I get this lip gloss? I'll use my own money. Pleeeease?"

"Will you *ever* let me wear makeup?"

When I was thirteen, I constantly pestered my mother with these questions. After reading teen magazines, I was convinced that makeup was what I needed to be beautiful. Just a little mascara, a bit of blush, and a dab of lip gloss, and I would be able to look like the models on the glossy pages I read over and over. A few cosmetics were all I needed to make everyone at school like me—to make *me* like me.

Judging by the thousands of beauty products available, I'm not the only one who has ever had those thoughts. During a quick trip to the drugstore today, I stopped to browse in the makeup aisle, and I was astounded by the number of mascaras available for sale. Under the Maybelline sign alone, I counted twelve different tubes of the stuff. Almay had five. Cover Girl had thirteen. In all, I found seventy-three unique products guaranteed to enhance my eyelashes!

That doesn't even take into account all of the other items offered in the cosmetic aisle. We can buy products to make our cheeks appear rosier, our eyebrows darker, and our lips shinier. Thousands of choices are available to buff up our appearance—our physical beauty.

But even when I looked up and down all the aisles of the store, I couldn't find any products to help me enhance my inner beauty. I didn't see any gels or lotions to help me develop a beautiful heart.

Which is sad, because that's the kind of beauty God wants us to have. In the Book of 1 Peter, He tells us:

> Do not let your adorning be external—the braiding of hair
> and the putting on of gold jewelry, or the clothing you
> wear—but let your adorning be the hidden person of the
> heart with the imperishable beauty of a gentle and quiet
> spirit, which in God's sight is very precious.
> 1 Peter 3:3–4

It seems that even two thousand years ago, women struggled with this inner and outer beauty thing. The women to whom the apostle Peter was writing were braiding their hair, wearing fancy clothes, and buying expensive jewelry in order to improve their appearance.

Now, I don't think that Peter was telling these women that it was wrong to fix their hair or wear nice clothes. He isn't saying we shouldn't wear makeup or put on a necklace. I think he was telling them—telling *us*—that the latest hairstyle or the trendiest wardrobe isn't what makes a girl lovely. True beauty comes from inside.

Although the magazines, television commercials, and celebrity shows will try to convince us otherwise, relying on outward beauty for our self-worth is a waste of time because:

Pursuing beauty is hopeless. External beauty isn't lasting. The cover-girl look lasts only until it rubs off on the washcloth.

Striving for beauty will always leave us feeling we are never quite lovely enough. Trying to look like the celebrities in magazine photos is impossible. Even the models themselves don't look like the pictures without the help of Photoshop.

Chasing after beauty will lead only to an empty and meaningless life. I have a lovely grand piano in my living room, but if I spend all my time polishing its shiny ebony finish without ever taking the time to play it, I am ignoring the purpose of the piano—to make music. If we spend all our time trying to perfect our outward beauty, we are missing the purpose for which God made us. He created us to experience His love and acceptance and share it with the world—this is what makes our souls shine with inner beauty that only God can give.

God tells us that instead of seventy-three tubes of mascara, instead of hundreds of cosmetics, there is only one thing we need to be truly beautiful: faith in Jesus, which shines with the beauty of a gentle and quiet spirit.

The New Testament wasn't originally written in English, of course. Peter wrote in Greek. And the Greek word used for *gentle* in 1 Peter 3:4 means having a graceful soul.

The word *quiet* in this passage describes a peaceful heart that is not upset by chaotic circumstances. It has a tranquility that isn't dependent on having a perfect day. Obviously there is chaos and there are imperfect days, but the Holy Spirit encourages us to still trust God. The person with the quiet heart is the one who manages to remain calm and clean during a cafeteria food fight.

This doesn't mean that we are timid or that we pathetically sit in a corner all day, never talking to our friends. It means that we trust God to work through His gifts to us, even "the unfading beauty of a gentle and quiet spirit."

Basically, God gives us permission to be calm. Even in the ugliness and chaos of this world, Scripture encourages us so that we may trust Him from the heart.

Although there aren't any products available in the cosmetics aisle to give us gentle and quiet hearts, we don't have to lose hope. God is more than willing to give us what we need to be able to hold His hand in trust when we start to question what's happening in our lives. He sent His Son—He isn't holding back! And He sent us His Spirit to quiet down our chaotic hearts.

I think our heavenly Father seriously wonders why we expect bottles of liquids and tubes of gels to give us worth and beauty. Because He has already done that.

God has made us beautiful.

> *Heavenly Father, please forgive me for the times I have been too concerned about hairstyles, makeup, and clothes. Help me to focus on the beauty of Your Son in my life. Give me the gentle and quiet spirit that will make me lovely in Your eyes. In Jesus' name. Amen.*

Your inner beauty never needs makeup.

If you know that God thinks you're beautiful, that's all that matters.
Leah

Day Three
◇◇◇◇◇◇◇◇◇◇◇◇◇◇◇◇◇◇◇◇◇◇◇◇
Wardrobe Workout

1. In 2012, teenager Julia Bluhm petitioned *Seventeen* magazine to print one unaltered photo in each issue. She said, "I've always just known how Photoshop can have a big effect on girls and their body image and how they feel about themselves. You need to see something realistic—you need to see a reflection of what truly represents a teenage girl nowadays."[1] What do you think? How do the unrealistic photos in today's magazines affect how you see yourself?

2. How do you define inner beauty? What are some of the characteristics of girls you know who shine from the inside out?

3. Read 1 Peter 3:1–6. This passage is a little tutorial on inner beauty.

   a. What qualities of inner beauty does Peter mention in verse 2?

   b. Verses 5 and 6 talk about how women of the past who were beautiful in God's eyes. Look at the end of verse 6. How can we follow their example?

c. In verse 4, Peter writes, "Let your adorning be the hidden person of the heart." Your external beauty routine may include shampoo, curling iron, makeup, and wardrobe. If you had a routine to beautify your heart, what might it include?

4. Get a close-up. Zoom in on one thing you discovered today.

5. Write out this week's memory verse. Try to do it without looking back at the words.

Day Four

◇◇◇◇◇◇◇◇◇◇◇◇◇◇◇◇◇◇◇◇

Out With the Old

But now you must put them all away: anger, wrath, malice,
slander, and obscene talk from your mouth. Do not lie to
one another, seeing that you have put off the old self with
its practices. Colossians 3:8—9

I am a sweater-holic. I can't help it. I live in Chicago, where—if it's not one of the twelve days of the year when it's so hot that you want to stuff ice packs down your clothes—you need sweaters.

Plus, shopping for sweaters is fun. They come in a gazillion colors and styles. I can buy them in oodles of patterns and textures. I can spend a lot and buy a cashmere sweater at Macy's or pay a little for a cute cotton one at Target. Maybe best of all, I can buy tons of them for almost nothing at the thrift store.

There is only one problem with the last option.

When I come home from the resale store with twenty new-to-me sweaters, I have to find a place to put them. But my closet is already full. My dresser drawers are already stuffed.

If I want to keep my new sweaters, I have to get rid of some of the old. And sometimes it is difficult for me to part with some of my favorite garments.

Never mind that I never even wear some of them. That the wool pullover is too scratchy. Or that when I got that blue cardigan home, it simply didn't look as cute as it did in the store. Or that I completely forgot about the teal turtleneck because it was buried under a dozen other sweaters.

I start to toss them into a giveaway pile, but then I stop myself. Perhaps I could wear a T-shirt under the itchy pullover. Maybe the blue one would work with a belt. And the teal turtleneck? I just have to put it on the top of the pile.

Cleaning out my closet isn't always easy.

The truth is, cleaning out my spiritual closet isn't always a cinch either. God tells us that we need to get rid of some things in our lives:

> Put to death therefore what is earthly in you: sexual immorality, impurity, passion, evil desire, and covetousness, which is idolatry. On account of these the wrath of God is coming. In these you too once walked, when you were living in them. But now you must put them all away: anger, wrath, malice, slander, and obscene talk from your mouth. Do not lie to one another, seeing that you have put off the old self with its practices. Colossians 3:5–9

But I start to rationalize. Those are seriously major sins. Me? I don't really need to change. I only told a little lie. So what if envy over my friend's popularity is eating me up? Everyone uses a little bad language now and then; who cares?

God cares. And not for the reason you might think. We tend to think of God as a scorekeeper. Do a good deed—get ten points. Say a bad word—get a penalty.

Our heavenly Father has given us rules. But He didn't give us these rules to make our lives miserable. We are to follow His Commandments because they reveal the Divine Designer of our lives.

Colossians 3:5 says, "Put to death therefore what is earthly in you." The part of us that is stained with sin doesn't actually fit us, although Satan will always try to convince us that it does. He will urge us to try on envy, obscene talk, even promiscuity, promising us that this is what an attractive life is all about. But eventually, we discover the ugly truth: sin kills and destroys the beauty of our souls.

God has designed us for something better. He is ready to give us the spiritual clothes that fit us perfectly and make us feel better than ever before. He has prepared custom-made fashions that will make us feel both lovely and loved in His Son, Jesus Christ.

Although I may continue to struggle to part with some of my old sweaters, I pray that I won't become so attached to the world that I don't want something better. I pray that God would give me a glimpse of the vision He has for my life so that I don't settle for anything less.

Our heavenly Designer is like an expert wardrobe consultant who sees our potential for beauty. Like a makeover artist who can envision a client looking ten times more attractive than she is now, God is able to see us at our best. His plan for our lives is more wonderful than we can ever imagine.

Father in heaven, too often I have attempted to fit into this world. I have tried on many things that have only ended up being uncomfortable and unattractive. I thank You that You have a wonderful vision for my life. Give me the strength to throw out the old. Clothe me in Your beauty. In Jesus' name. Amen.

Throw Out the Old

Cleaning out your closet can be a difficult and depressing job. To make it more fun, team up with a friend. Ask her to help you decide which clothes look great on you and which you should toss. After you are done with your closet, go work on hers. Maybe you can even exchange a few outfits!

Day Four
Wardrobe Workout

1. We all hang on to ugly attitudes or behaviors. List some reasons why it's hard to clean out our spiritual closets.

2. Read Colossians 3:5–9 again. Verse 5 tells us we are to put off idolatry. In this modern world, most of us don't worship gold statues, but that doesn't mean we don't have idols. An idol is anything in our life that we treat as more important than God. Using that definition, what are some modern-day idols?

3. Get a close-up. Zoom in on one thing you discovered today.

4. Write out this week's memory verse. No peeking!

Study Styles

I love to dig into Scripture. To get the most out of my study time, I use a variety of ways to discover what God is saying in His Word. In this section, I will introduce you to different techniques for exploring the Bible. Each week, we will try a new study style.

One good way to get the most out of your Bible study is to make charts of what you have learned. Using Colossians 3:5–17, fill out the chart of What Not to Wear/What to Wear.

What Not to Wear

_____

_____

_____

_____

_____

What to Wear

_____

_____

_____

_____

_____

Now circle the characteristics you are currently wearing!

Day Five

<><><><><><><><><><><><><><><><><><><><>

Change Your Clothes

Put on the new self, which is being renewed in knowledge
after the image of its creator. Colossians 3:10

Christmas was coming. I had purchased most of my gifts. But there was still one person I needed to shop for—my father.

I never knew what to get my dad. It seemed an impossible task to find something he actually wanted or needed. I asked my mother what she thought he might like for Christmas. She said, "He could use some new flannel shirts for wearing around the house. The ones he has are really torn and ratty." So I went to Sears, bought two thick, warm, colorful flannel shirts, and wrapped them in red and green paper, anticipating a smile on my father's face when he unwrapped the package.

But when my father opened the box, he said, "Why do I need these? I already have a whole drawer full of new flannel shirts!" My dad kept wearing the old, ratty shirts even though he had brand-new ones available.

Sometimes we are that way with our spiritual clothing as well. We learn all about new fashions for our soul, but we keep wearing the old ones. God offers us beautiful new garments, yet we continue to put on the unattractive ones we have grown used to. Like my dad with his shirts, we store our new character in a drawer for someday in the future.

This week we have already learned about the essential garments of salvation and righteousness. We have explored the difference between outward and inner beauty. We have seen that God wants us to get rid of the old because He has a beautiful new vision for our lives.

Colossians 3:10 talks about this new vision, the new person God wants to fashion us into:

> Put on the new self, which is being renewed in knowledge
> after the image of its creator.

Did you notice that the word *new* appears twice in this short little verse? First, God tells us to put on the *new* self, and then He tells us that this self is being renewed.

When I am studying Scripture, one of the things I like to do is look up words in the original languages of the Bible. The New Testament was written in Greek, so I searched for these two words in a Greek dictionary. It turns out that the words translated *new* in Colossians 3:10 are from two different Greek words. The first one, in the phrase "the new self," is translated from the Greek word *neos* and means new in relation to time. This is like the new flannel shirts I bought for my dad. He already had flannel shirts, but he had worn them for a long time. I bought the same kind of shirts, but they didn't have the holes the old ones did. Another example of this "new" might be if your favorite Skechers wore out and you bought the exact same Skechers, only newer.

The second *new* in the word *renewed* is *anakainos* in the Greek. The root word is *kainos*, which means new in relation to quality. If I had bought my father *kainos* new shirts, I would not have purchased $15 flannel shirts like he often wore. I would have splurged on a custom-tailored, polished-cotton shirt with French cuffs. If you were buying *kainos* new shoes, you wouldn't simply replace your worn Skechers. You would shop for a brand-new pair of Jimmy Choos.

On our own, we can only put on the *neos* new. We can brush on mascara and style our hair. We can buy new clothes and refashion our image. We can even try to change our behavior by reading self-help books or making New Year's resolutions. Still, inside, we are the same person.

But when God works His makeover miracles, we become *kainos* new. He transforms us from the inside out. He alters the quality of our character and the value of our lives. In fact, the change is so dramatic that we begin to look like our Designer. Colossians says that we are being renewed in the image of our Creator.

I wish I could say that my divine makeover is complete, that I already look just like my heavenly Father. But I still mess up. I still make mistakes. I still wear my old self sometimes. It's then that God reminds me I am *being* renewed. It is a continual process. And it can be a process of joy and discovery.

Picture Jesus coming to your closet. But instead of the closet being full of your usual clothes, it contains some of the attitudes and behaviors that you've been meaning to toss. Jesus looks at you and gently asks, "Are you ready to change?"

You hesitate, but Jesus takes your hands in His own nail-scarred hands and reassures you. "You are beautiful, My daughter. But some of the things you've been wearing are ruining your image. They're holding you back from being the person you are created to be. They've become comfortable because you have worn them so long. But I have something even better in mind. Will you trust Me? Will you take the next step to become a better you?" You nod your head, and Jesus begins to pull out clothes you are a little embarrassed for Him to see. But with each item, it becomes easier to watch Him toss them into the trash can. Just when you think the process is finished, Jesus brings an armload of beautiful new clothes for you to wear. He picks up a jacket and holds it out to you. You slip it on. You are amazed. It fits perfectly. When you catch a glimpse of yourself in the mirror, you can't believe it's you. Somehow the color and the fit of the jacket make you look ten times better than you usually do. You feel beautiful.

Jesus smiles and whispers, "You look lovely, My princess."

Heavenly Designer, only You can make me new. Only You can transform me from the inside out. Help me to come to You each day for the next step in my divine makeover. Thank You that You are working to change me into Your image. Amen.

Controlling Your Closet

Organize your closet by hanging like things together. Arrange clothes by color and type. Hang all the red shirts together, all the blue pants together, and so forth. It will help you find the outfit you want on those mornings when you can barely open your eyes.

31

Day Five
◇◇◇◇◇◇◇◇◇◇◇◇◇◇◇◇◇◇◇◇◇◇
Wardrobe Workout

1. Reread the last four paragraphs of today's reading.

   a. Is there anything that makes you uncomfortable when you read the description of Jesus cleaning out your spiritual closet?

   b. Is there anything in that description that gives you joy?

2. What does a divine makeover mean to you? What changes would you like to see in your life?

3. Read Colossians 3:12.

   a. How does that verse describe us?

   b. How does knowing that is how God sees you help you to step out into a divine makeover?

4. Get a close-up. Zoom in on one thing you discovered today.

5. Write out this week's memory verse, Ephesians 4:22, 24 from memory.

Meaningful Makeover

Bible study is more than learning facts and terms. God's Word is living and active and transforms our lives. Look at the chart you completed yesterday (page 28). Choose one item you circled in the "What Not to Wear" column that you would like to toss or one item not circled in the "What to Wear" column that you would like to add to your life. What are some steps you can take to make this a reality? (For instance: I would like to make a more conscious effort to be kind. One way I could do this would be to send encouraging cards or emails to my friends.)

Write a prayer asking your divine Designer to help you edit out the unattractive behavior or to clothe you with one that will reflect your new image in Christ.

Remember to bring the clothing item from
Day One to your group's meeting!

Fashion
Finesse

A few words about finding the right clothes, building a wardrobe, and looking your best

Modesty Myths and Truths

"Modest is hottest."

"There's nothing wrong with dressing a little sexy."

"Real Christians don't wear miniskirts."

"Looking hot is the way to get a guy."

Modesty is a hot topic. But it's not one that everyone agrees on.

What exactly is modesty?

First, let's look at what modesty is *not* by exploring three myths of modesty:

Modesty Myth #1: Modesty is old-fashioned.

Imagine what might happen if a teenager from the 1800s could visit a modern-day mall. Would she cover her gaping mouth with her daintily gloved hand when she saw what today's teens were wearing? Would she shield her eyes with a fluttering fan? or gather up her long skirts and run away?

It's true that fashions in previous eras provided much more coverage. But although high collars and floor-length dresses may have gone out of style, that doesn't mean modesty has.

Modesty is an enduring principle. In 1 Timothy 2:9, we read this:

Women should adorn themselves in respectable apparel, with modesty and self-control.

In other words, God's timeless Word tells us to wear modest clothing, not drawing attention to ourselves by the way we dress. Because
God's Word never goes out of style, this verse is not fashion advice
for first-century women only. It is for all of us.

Modesty Myth #2: Modesty means dressing in a burlap bag.

Okay, when you became a teenager, your father probably wished he
could buy you a set of shapeless sacks in different colors in order to
hide your beauty. But dressing modestly doesn't necessarily mean that
we can't wear the latest styles. It does mean that we have to make
wise choices when deciding which trends to follow and which to avoid.

It may mean adapting styles: wearing a camisole under a too-low top,
adding leggings to a dress that's a bit too short, wearing a cute jacket
or sweater over a top that's either too sheer or too tight. We can use
our God-given creativity to dress stylishly *and* modestly.

Modesty Myth #3: Modesty means following a strict set of clothing rules.

When I was a fourth grader, miniskirts were the new fashion trend. But
the Christian school I attended was determined to monitor this trend
and not let the miniskirts get too mini. The eleventh commandment
that year was "Thou shalt not have a skirt shorter than three inches
above the knee."

Maybe you have seen similar modesty rules—rules that tell you how
low is too low, how tight is too tight, how sheer is too sheer. And
while some guidelines might be helpful, the problem with rules is that
they tend to lead to even more rules. They tend to lead to an atmo-
sphere of judgmental attitudes.

Instead of rules, modesty means following a heart attitude of dressing with an attitude of respect: respect for the beauty God gave you;
respect for God's Word, which instructs us to dress modestly; respect
for the gift of sexuality, which God has reserved for the intimate bond
of marriage.

Now that we have discussed what modesty *isn't*, let's talk about what modesty *is*. Here are three modesty truths:

Modesty Truth #1: Modesty is safeguarding your most intimate beauty for one man—your husband.

Dressing provocatively is like giving the treasure map to every guy you know when, in reality, you want only one faithful man to find that treasure. By covering up your most private beauty, you are protecting your valuable treasure for the one who will love you like no one else. God wants you to see yourself as a precious jewel that requires special care. And although marriage may seem a long way off, your future husband will appreciate your efforts to reserve your intimate beauty.

Modesty Truth #2: Modesty means knowing that your body is a temple of the Holy Spirit.

In God's view, our bodies are much more than clothes hangers. 1 Corinthians 6:19–20 tells us:

Do you not know that your body is a temple of the Holy Spirit within you, whom you have from God? You are not your own, for you were bought with a price. So glorify God in your body.

Your body is more than skin and bone; it is a temple of the Holy Spirit. Jesus paid the high price of His own life to make you His very own. How you dress reflects on the God who has taken up residence in your body.

Modesty Truth #3: Modesty is realizing that your worth does not come from the attention guys may shower on you, but from the almighty God choosing you to be His daughter.

Let's face it: when you watch the eyes of all the guys in the room follow the girl in the short skirt, it's tempting to want some of that attention. But you don't have to sacrifice your modesty in order to be noticed. Listen to what God tells you in His Word: "You are precious in My eyes, and honored, and I love you" (Isaiah 43:4). Think about it. You don't need to catch the eyes of a bunch of guys because God's eyes are constantly following you. In His eyes, you have always been treasured. To the almighty God, you are priceless.

Modesty is realizing your value in Christ and dressing in a way that honors Him and the beauty He gave you.

Modesty means knowing you're beautiful inside and out without having to prove it to others.

Some questions to ask yourself:

- How does remembering that my body is a temple of the Holy Spirit change my choice of clothes?

- When I was picking out my clothes today, whose attention was I trying to get?

- Since God thinks I'm beautiful, how can I honor Him by the way I dress?

WEEK TWO

Hang Up the Uniform and Let Go of Your Inner Control Freak

Memory Verse

I delight to do Your will, O my God; Your law is within my heart. Psalm 40:8

Day One
◇◇◇◇◇◇◇◇◇◇
In Control

Submit yourselves therefore to God. James 4:7

"Sharla, you definitely would be classified as a Field Marshal."

My sister-in-law's words caught me off guard. I was sitting at the dinner table enjoying a relaxed meal with my extended family. We were passing potatoes and sharing stories when my sister-in-law began talking about a personality test she was using at work. She was so excited about the test that she started to guess how each of us might be classified.

She went around the table, identifying each person: "You would probably be called a Mastermind." "I think you would be a Champion." "You might be a Healer."

As she went from person to person, I wondered what I might be. Mastermind and Champion sounded impressive. But when my sister-in-law looked at me and called me a Field Marshal, I was stunned. How could she compare me to a bossy military commander who ordered people around?

Was she right? Did other people perceive me as bossy and controlling? Although I wasn't convinced that *I* was the one wearing a field marshal uniform, my sister-in-law's comment forced me to look at myself.

Well, I did like to keep things organized. Like an army officer, I took charge of my surroundings: clothes arranged by color, kitchen utensils by use, and books by author's last name. But did that make me a control freak?

Okay, maybe I wore that field marshal uniform more often than I wanted to admit. I knew that my inner control freak often came out when I was working with others. I can't help offering suggestions: "Don't you think it would be better if we did it this way?" "I've found this method to be much more successful." "I really don't think that's right."

Then I realized that I sometimes did the same thing with my heavenly Father: "God, my life would be so much better if You answered my prayers according to my plan." "This is *not* the way my life should be going!"

When I looked at myself honestly, I couldn't deny I had a few control issues. So I took my sister-in-law's words to heart and tried to change my ways. I realized that my relationships with God and the people in my life could be improved if I took off the commander's uniform.

If we're truthful, we all like to be in control. Maybe you find yourself in charge of every school or class project. Or you might feel the need to dictate what you and your friends do every Saturday night. Perhaps your inner control freak demands that you keep everything you own in perfect order. One especially organized teenager I talked to joked that she called her version of obsessive-compulsive disorder "CDO" because "OCD" isn't alphabetical.

When we're ready to change, the first step is realizing that God is the one wearing the field marshal uniform. James 4:7 says, "Submit yourselves therefore to God." The Greek word for *submit* is actually a military term meaning "to rank under." In other words, if I am submitting to God, I am willing to obey Him. Instead of wearing the powerful commander's uniform, I have to be willing to put on the common soldier's fatigues. I am the one who takes orders, not gives them.

Okay, I admit this is not easy, especially for someone who is a Field Marshal. It goes against everything in me to let God be in charge of my life. I want things to go *my* way.

But then I remember: God is God and I am not. No matter how badly I want to control the universe to my advantage, the truth is, God is in control. When I pull against His leading, I am only struggling to get out of His loving hand.

A surprising thing happens when I stop resisting and allow my heavenly Father to lead me. When I let Him direct my life, I find that I'm happier than when I think I'm the one in charge. When I stop pounding my fists and demanding my way, I can open up my hands for God's blessings.

After my sister-in-law called me a Field Marshal, I made an effort to resist putting on that uniform. It wasn't easy, but I began to use phrases like "You decide" and "It's your choice." I think that at first, my family and friends were a little stunned to hear those words come out of my mouth, but over time, saying those words has become more natural for me.

But the real change comes when we allow God to be the commander of our lives. We can experience an unexplainable freedom when we tell Him, "Father, I want what *You* want for my life." When we are ready to take off that field marshal uniform, God is ready to guide us to a divine design.

Lord Jesus, I admit that I have not always treated You as the Lord of my life. Too often I have tried to be in control. But now I'm ready to let You be the commander. I'm willing to take Your hand and let You lead. Amen.

Are You a Field Marshal Too?

You might be a Field Marshal if:

• you always seem to be the one in charge of projects.

• you are quick to take the lead.

• you are a natural goal setter.

• you need to express your opinions to the group.

Being a Field Marshal isn't all bad. Field Marshals are devoted to their work and make good administrators and executives.[2]

Day One
Wardrobe Workout

1. Do you wear a uniform for school or work? Or do you have an outfit that gives you an extra boost of confidence? How does wearing that uniform or outfit make you feel? If you are doing this study in a group, bring that outfit to your group meeting. Talk about how what we wear can affect how we look at ourselves.

2. If you were given a choice, which would you rather wear: the field marshal's uniform or the private's uniform? In other words, do you see yourself more as a leader or a follower? Why?

3. If God is in charge of my life, then I must obey His commands. Read the following passages. What does God say about obedience and following His commands?

   a. Isaiah 48:18

   b. Jeremiah 7:23

   c. 1 John 5:3

4. Get a close-up. Zoom in on one thing you discovered today.

5. Our memory verse for this week is Psalm 40:8: "I delight to do Your will, O my God; Your law is within my heart." To help you memorize this passage, try *Scripture Typer* (scripturetyper.com); it's a fun way to use your computer or phone to commit the Bible to memory. Also, write the passage out in the space below.

Day Two

◇◇◇◇◇◇◇

Let Go

He said to all, "If anyone would come after Me,
let him deny himself and take up his cross daily
and follow Me." Luke 9:23

A crowd was gathering around Mr. Larson's office. Everyone was push-ing forward, straining to see the lists posted on his office window. I pushed up on my tiptoes to see above all the other heads, praying that my name would be on the list of people who made it into the best choir in the school.

But my name was not on the roster of the Concert Choir.

Before the auditions, I had been confident of my chances of making the top choir. But the day of my audition, I had come down with a cold and didn't sing my best. Now I would be stuck in the second-rate choir for another year.

This was especially disappointing to me because I had been thinking about my future. Perhaps I could major in music when I went to college. But with Mr. Larson's verdict, I realized that if I was not talented enough to get into the high school Concert Choir, then I had no business thinking about majoring in music in college. I did what any disappointed teenager would do: I cried into my pillow for days.

But through the tears, I also asked God why. I had prayed that I would make it into the Concert Choir. Why had God answered that prayer with a no?

After I spent a few days listening, I realized something that I didn't want to hear. My dreams and ambitions had become more important to me than my relationship to Him. In the quiet corners of my heart, I heard Him ask me to give up music.

Although I didn't completely understand this whole concept of let-ting go, it was clear that my goals were creating a wedge between God and me. So I placed my decade of piano lessons, years of singing, and dreams of becoming a professional musician in His hands.

A curious thing happened. Even as tears rolled down my cheeks, peace piled up in my heart.

This was my first experience with what Jesus called "denying yourself." Jesus told His disciples:

> If anyone would come after Me, let him deny himself and take up his cross daily and follow Me. For whoever would save his life will lose it, but whoever loses his life for My sake will save it. For what does it profit a man if he gains the whole world and loses or forfeits himself? (Luke 9:23–25)

This all sounds very confusing. How can I find myself by denying myself? How can I save my life by losing it? This concept is totally opposite my human thinking. It makes much more sense to pursue what I want at all costs.

But girls, this is one of the most important lessons we can ever learn. When we let go of our ideas about how our life should go, we discover that God's vision for our lives is bigger than anything we could dream of. When we remember all that He has already done for us, we can trust Him to deliver an amazing future.

Not all of our sacrifices will be huge. Perhaps God is asking you to give up a favorite television show so you will have more time to read His Word. Maybe He is nudging you to abandon a friendship that is leading you away from His path for your life. Perhaps you could sacrifice something you want to do and instead help your parents or play with your siblings. It could be that He is guiding you to give up some free time in order to serve your church or community.

Sometimes surrender is simply the act of accepting where God has placed you now. If your life is not going according to your Plan A, denying yourself is trusting that God knows what He is doing. If your dreams have been crushed, losing yourself is believing that God's dreams for you are better than your own.

That's what I experienced when I trusted God's vision for my life and let go of my own ambitions. A few days after I gave God all of my musical hopes and dreams, I felt a nudge to ask Mr. Larson for a second audition. I decided to tell him that I had a cold the day of the tryouts and see if he would give me a second chance. Well, Mr. Larson did give me a new audition—*and* a spot in the Concert Choir. I was thrilled that God had answered my prayer with a yes.

But God's dreams for me were even bigger than my own. A few days later, one of my friends, a fellow musician, approached me in the hall with an invitation to play the keyboard percussion (instruments like the xylophone, bells, and marimba) in the band. The idea of playing in the band had never entered my mind, but it was in God's plan all along.

In the coming years, God continued to surprise me. During my last two years of high school, I was not only part of the Concert Choir and Concert Band, but I also was given the opportunity to participate in the orchestra and an elite group of singers called the Chamber Choir. After high school, I toured the country for a year with a Christian singing group. And, yes, after that, I went to college and graduated with a music degree. Today, I use my talent to teach others and to praise God in the worship service at church.

Giving up control of our lives doesn't seem logical at first. And letting go of our own ideas about how life should be doesn't mean that we should sit back and just let things happen. God still expects us to use our talents, our intellect, and our opportunities for the good of others and to His glory. After all, He's the one who gave us our one-of-a-kind lives. We should still try our best on the next big test, for example, or the next tryout. In my case, I knew I had a gift for music, so I tried again. But if I had abandoned that gift and instead decided to keep crying in my pillow, then I would have failed to use my God-given ability.

What I needed to do was stop focusing on what *I* thought was best for my life and think about what God wanted me to do with the gifts He had given me. I needed to just trust Him and understand that when we place all of our plans in the Father's loving hands, He is there to take those goals and turn them into something better than we can do on our own.

> *Lord Jesus, letting go isn't easy. I hang onto my hopes and dreams because I can't imagine my life any other way. Give me the strength to place them in Your hands. I trust Your goodness. I want Your plan for my life. Amen.*

Deny

To deny oneself is to let go of your own self-centered desires and to consider the interests of others.

When we are prepared to trust God, He is ready to surprise us with His goodness.

Day Two

◇◇◇◇◇◇◇◇◇◇◇◇◇◇◇◇◇◇◇◇◇◇◇◇

Wardrobe Workout

1. In today's reading, I talked about my love for music. What is one of your passions?

2. Read Luke 9:23–25.

   a. After reading today's lesson, what do you think it means to deny yourself?

   b. When the disciples followed Jesus, they gave up their careers, time with their families, some physical comforts, and even their lives. What might you have to give up to follow Jesus?

c. In verse 25, Jesus tells us that if we make it our goal to "[gain] the whole world"—to go after our earthly idea of success, money, fame—we are in danger of losing our true selves. How can chasing after earthly success change us? Have you seen this happen to anyone you know? any celebrities?

3. Get a close-up. Zoom in on one thing you discovered today.

4. Write out our memory verse for this week: "I delight to do Your will, O my God; Your law is within my heart" (Psalm 40:8). Read a phrase, then cover it and write it. Try to write as much of the verse as you can without looking.

Day Three
◇◇◇◇◇◇◇◇◇◇◇◇◇◇◇◇◇◇
Like a Princess

I delight to do Your will, O my God; Your law is within my heart. Psalm 40:8

Do your parents ever encourage you to try something new because they are certain you would love it? Do you ever protest because you are sure they are wrong?

One of my favorite photos of my children when they were small is of the two of them standing at the front door, ready to go trick-or-treating for Halloween. Anna was dressed like a little princess and was clearly excited about going door-to-door to get treats. Nathaniel, however, was about to cry, even though I had made him a Thomas the Tank Engine costume so he could dress like his favorite toy. Nathaniel was only three and had never gone trick-or-treating before. He was sure that he would hate the whole experience. But when he came back with a bag full of candy, he was all smiles.

We had urged Nathaniel to try something new, not to torture him, but because we knew that once he knocked on that first door and got that first handful of candy, he would love it.

Our memory verse this week is Psalm 40:8:

> I delight to do Your will, O my God; Your law is within my heart.

I don't know about you, but I can't always say "I delight to do Your will, O my God," and mean it. Often I'm sure that what God is asking me to do is going to make me miserable. Like my three-year-old son on that first Halloween, I can't envision anything good coming out of what God wants.

My attitude only gets worse when I examine the verse more closely. The word for *will* in the psalm means "delight, desire, or pleasure." In other words, the psalmist is saying, "God, I desire what *You* desire. I want to do whatever makes *You* happy."

Right away, my old self argues, "Are you kidding? Doing what someone else wants is going to give me a good life?" Satan tries to convince me that it is much more logical to say, "I delight to do *my* will. I want to do whatever makes *me* happy."

Our culture, too, constantly sends out messages that encourage us to do what makes us feel good: "Do whatever feels right. Think about what you need. Do whatever it takes to get what you want." We hear this in subtle and not-so-subtle forms in the songs we listen to, the shows we watch, and the commercials we are constantly bombarded with.

So why should we ignore these messages? Why should we shut out all the sources telling us to do exactly as we please?

Because God truly is like the loving parent urging His child to go out trick-or-treating. The prize that awaits us is eternal life through Jesus. He knows that prize will be there at the end of the day because He designed it that way.

Remember that picture of my children? my son wearing the train costume and my daughter dressed like a princess? I often act like the boy in the Thomas the Tank Engine costume—pouting because I'm sure that I will be miserable if I obey my Father. But God asks me to be more like the girl in the princess costume, because, in reality, that is what I am—a daughter of the King! And the King wants only what is best for His princess. He has spectacular plans for my life. He has castles full of blessings and towers stuffed with eternal wealth. He wants me to experience His treasures, love, and joy. The King asks me only to trust His wisdom.

Psalm 40 also tells us, "Blessed is the man who makes the LORD his trust" (v. 4). The King wants us to know that when we step out in obedience, He will reward us with bags of blessings. He promises to give His best gifts to those who act out of faith in His goodness.

And you know what? Every time we take a step of trust, it gets a little easier. That Halloween, my son learned that just maybe, Mom and Dad knew what they were talking about when they said he would have fun if he dressed up in a cute costume and visited the neighbors. It sounded strange, but it was true. And the next time we told him that a new experience would be fun, he was a little more likely to believe us.

Can we agree that, more than maybe, God knows what He is talking about when He says that His way is best? His way may seem unfamiliar, mysterious, and even downright weird, but each time we obey, we find that He is right.

So let's dress like God's princesses and discover that we truly do have more happiness when we delight in God's will. Let's step out as daughters of the King and realize that He loves us enough to give us His best.

> *My Father, my King, please forgive me when I doubt*
> *Your love for me and question Your path for my life. Help*
> *me to step out in faith and delight in Your will, trusting*
> *that it's also the way to happiness for me. In Jesus' name.*
> *Amen.*

We are all princesses, so we should act like it.
  Grace

If you are a princess, you want to bring honor to the King's name.
  Maddie

If you are a princess, you demand respect. You don't let other people treat you like dirt.
  Leah

Day Three
Wardrobe Workout

1. Can you think of a time in your life when you discovered that your parents really did know what was good for you? What was that time and what did you learn?

2. Because our heavenly Father is also King of the universe, we truly are princesses. How does that fact help you to do what God wants you to do?

3. Read Psalm 40:1–8. This psalm talks about what God asks us to do and what He promises to do for us.

   a. List some of the things God wants us to do.

   b. Which of these things is God asking you to do today? (For instance: I have been praying for something for a long time. Today, God is asking me to wait patiently [v. 1].)

   c. List some of the things God promises to do for us.

   d. Which of these things means the most to you today? (For instance: I am amazed that God has planned many wonders for my life [v. 5]!)

4. Get a close-up. Zoom in on one thing you discovered today.

5. Write out this week's memory verse. Try to do it without looking back at the words.

Day Four
<><><><><><><>
Judgment

Judge not, that you be not judged. For with the judgment
you pronounce you will be judged, and with the measure
you use it will be measured to you. Matthew 7:1–2

"Did you see what she's wearing?"

"That skirt is so last year."

"I can't believe she would go out in public in that outfit!"

You've probably heard conversations like this at the mall, in your school, maybe even at church. Perhaps the subject was someone's hairstyle or whom they were seen with on Saturday night, but the effect was the same:

Judgment.

It's easy to do. I've already admitted that I struggle to take off that field marshal uniform—I like to have things done my way. And when I find something that works for me, I tend to think everyone else should do it that way too. Sometimes what comes out of my mouth makes me sound like I've appointed myself chief critic of the universe.

Often what we judge are superficial things. We criticize someone's makeup, hair, or weight. We pronounce someone else's clothes up to our standards or completely unacceptable.

Those judgments hurt, but often our criticism goes deeper. We make fun of someone's disability or obvious lack of money. We accept those who are like us and shun those who aren't.

Sometimes as Christians we feel we have the right to judge because we know God's standards. We have memorized the Ten Commandments. God's Word explains what is right and what is wrong. We can see mistakes a mile away. Maybe we even feel it is our job to point out those mistakes.

But God tells us that is not our responsibility. Jesus told His disciples:

> Judge not, that you be not judged. For with the judgment
> you pronounce you will be judged, and with the measure
> you use it will be measured to you. Matthew 7:1–2

Did you catch that? We will be judged in the same way we judge others. Ouch! I don't think I could stand in front of Jesus and say, "Okay. I'm ready to be judged. Just treat me like I've treated the people in my life."

Jesus goes on to say:

> Why do you see the speck that is in your brother's eye, but do not notice the log that is in your own eye? Or how can you say to your brother, "Let me take the speck out of your eye," when there is the log in your own eye? You hypocrite, first take the log out of your own eye, and then you will see clearly to take the speck out of your brother's eye. Matthew 7:3–5

Picture this: You notice your friend's eyeliner is a little crooked. The tiniest spot at the corner of her eye is slightly off. You want to point it out, help her fix it, but you've got your own makeup mess. A chunk of mascara has suddenly lodged itself in your eye. It's so painful that you can't even open that eyelid. But instead of taking care of your own problem, you keep telling your friend, "Let me fix your makeup." Even as tears run out of your eye and your mascara smears all over your face, you are insisting that she let you help her fix that tiny corner of eyeliner.

Of course, the point of the eye makeup story is that instead of paying attention to where other people are messing up, we are supposed to look at ourselves. Before we point out other people's mistakes and sins, we are to find out where we have flubbed. We are to discover where we have disobeyed God's instructions, then repent and be forgiven, before we go in love to help a friend find that same forgiveness.

Jesus said that what is in my sister's eye is only a speck and that what is in my eye is a log. Her slightly crooked eyeliner isn't nearly as bad as all my runny mascara. We tend to look at the mistakes of others as worse than our own. God tells us to take an honest look at ourselves—at God's Word—before we start judging others.

Remember: Jesus is Judge, but He is also Savior. Because He paid the price for our sins, He offers us grace—His free and generous and unconditional mercy, love, and acceptance. As we receive His grace at His Table of forgiveness (Communion), let's offer it to others. Let's stop pronouncing judgment on superficial things. Let's learn to accept people even if they're not just like us. Instead of looking at people through the lens of society's standards, let's try to look at them through God's loving eyes.

> *Jesus, help me to remember that You are the Judge of the world and I am not. Forgive me for the times I've been critical of others simply because of the way they dressed or how much money they had. Help me to see the people around me through Your eyes of love. Amen.*

Before You Judge

Superficial judgments prevent us from seeing what is under the surface. Before we criticize others, let's learn their stories. Maybe the annoying girl in algebra acts that way because she's insecure. Perhaps the painfully awkward guy has a disability. Maybe the obsessive flirt has never known love at home and is simply trying to find it anywhere she can. Ask God to help you see others through His eyes.

I live in a very "judge-ful" city. I've been in groups of friends that talk for hours on end, judging people.
Raelyn

Day Four
Wardrobe Workout

1. What has been your experience with mean-spirited judging? Have you been in the group that was pronouncing the judgments? Or were you the one who was judged? In either case, how did that make you feel?

2. Read Luke 6:37–38. These verses are very similar to the Matthew verses in today's readings.

   a. Compare the Luke verses with the Matthew verses. What differences to you see?

   b. List the action words in the Luke verses (for example: *judge*).

   c. Which of the actions above do you think God wants you to take today?

3. Get a close-up. Zoom in on one thing you discovered today.

4. Write out this week's memory verse. No peeking!

Study Styles

Examining a passage of the Bible in several different translations can help us to understand the passage better because each version will translate the Greek or Hebrew words in a slightly different way. Each version can help us to see the same idea from a new perspective, and when we put them together, we gain new insight.

Look up Luke 9:23 in several versions of the Bible. You don't have to own all the versions; you can use the Passage Lookup feature available with an online Bible like BibleGateway.com. You might want to look at some modern or contemporary versions to help you understand all the terms.

Write out each version of the verse and underline a phrase or word in each version that helps you to understand the passage.

a. Version used: _____

Luke 9:23 in this version

b. Version used: _____

Luke 9:23 in this version

c. Version used: _____
Luke 9:23 in this version

Now rewrite Luke 9:23 in your own "version" using your new understanding and perhaps your underlined words and phrases.

Day Five
◇◇◇◇◇◇◇◇◇◇◇◇◇◇◇◇◇◇◇◇
That Kind of Girl

Let every person be subject to the governing authorities.
For there is no authority except from God, and those that
exist have been instituted by God. Romans 13:1

Once upon a time, there were two sisters living in a lovely home in a quiet city. Both sisters had parents to love them, friends to play with, and a brother to tease them. But the two sisters had very different personalities. Sister A was quiet. Sister B had a voice that could be heard across the house. Sister A was shy. Sister B was outgoing. And when it came to obeying their parents, Sister A was an I'll-do-what-you-say-but-I-won't-like-it kind of girl. Sister B was an I-dare-you-to-make-me-do-what-you-want kind of girl.

One day, Sister A wanted to go to a movie with her friends. "Mom, everyone in our class is going to the movie on Friday night. Can I go too?"

The answer came immediately: "No way. I can't approve of that movie. You will not be going."

Sister A obeyed, but she pouted in her room all Friday night.

Later, Sister B wanted to go to a friend's house: "Mom, can I go over to Emily's house on Saturday night?"

This answer came a little slower, but it was still a *no*: "Sorry, but Emily is not a very good influence on you. You will not be going."

Sister B went to her room on Saturday night, but before she did, she placed a chair outside her window behind the bushes. While her parents thought she was sulking in her room, Sister B escaped through her window and headed to Emily's house.

You may have suspected that the story is really about my sister and me. I'll let you guess which sister I was!

While my sister and I had different responses to our parents' authority, we both agreed on one thing: we didn't like it. We wanted to be in control of our own lives. We couldn't wait to grow up so we could do what we wanted.

But it didn't take too long into our adult lives to realize that even when you are all grown up, you still can't always do exactly what you want to do. It seems there is always someone in charge, and it is usually not you. Sometimes we just want to be like Sister B and escape all the rules.

This is a natural human tendency. Ever since Eve broke the one rule in the Garden of Eden (see Genesis 3:1–7), we've been fighting against rules and trying to wriggle out of obeying laws.

It may surprise you to know that authority was God's idea. Romans 13:1–2 says:

> Let every person be subject to the governing authorities. For there is no authority except from God, and those that exist have been instituted by God. Therefore whoever resists the authorities resists what God has appointed, and those who resist will incur judgment.

To establish order in a messy world, God has placed certain people in charge. And unless those authorities ask us to do something against His Word, God expects us to obey them. They will ultimately have to speak to God about the way they have used that authority, but in the meantime, we are to obey.

Here are a few of the authorities in our lives:

Parents: If you are still living at home, you are to obey your parents. Although it may not seem like it, parents usually have more wisdom than their children. They may be aware of consequences of your actions that you can't see yet. And even if you are an adult and supporting yourself, the commandment "Honor your father and your mother" still applies to you. God wants us to treat our parents with respect whenever possible. (You may be asking, "But what if I don't have good parents?" If so, check out page 230.)

Bosses and teachers: God asks us to work for others like we are working for Him. He wants us to do our best, even when they are not looking (Colossians 3:23–24).

Public authorities: According to what we learned in Romans 13:1, presidents, governors, mayors, and policemen all have been given their authority by God. He asks us to obey them unless they tell us to do something against His Word. Thankfully, in this country, we have the privilege of working to change laws and voting to replace authorities that we don't agree with.

Although we might wish that we could be like Sister B and climb out the window to escape all the rules, it helps to remember that God has placed those rules in the world for a purpose. He put certain people in charge for our good and in order to make the world a less messy place. The King of the universe asks us to give up some of the control in our lives as we obey the laws. When we follow the leaders God has established, we are following Him and demonstrating our faith.

Dear almighty King, I have to be honest. Sometimes I just don't feel like obeying my parents or respecting the authorities. I just want to do what I want to do. Help me to see that You have placed certain people in charge for my own good. Help me to do my best to treat those people with respect. In Jesus' name. Amen.

Parents aren't perfect, but they want the best for their kids.
Grace

Rules vs. Chaos

God asks us to follow rules for our own good. Imagine that you had just passed your driver's test and were now the proud owner of a shiny new driver's license. However, something changed between the time you completed your road test and the moment you posed for your photo. When you came out of the DMV, you saw people were driving on both sides of the road, not paying any attention to traffic lights, and going as fast as they wanted. Would you want to get back into your car? If there were *no* rules, chaos would be in charge.

Day Five

Wardrobe Workout

1. Tell the truth: Are you more of a Sister A kind of girl or a Sister B kind of girl? How does that girl behave with your parents? your teachers? your friends?

2. Read Ephesians 5:21–6:9. This section of Scripture tells us to submit to certain people. The word *submit* means to take your proper role in God's order and lay down your selfish interests. Let's examine how that word is applied in different relationships.

   a. Why are we to submit to one another (5:21)? How does this make submitting easier?

   b. What is the reward for honoring our parents (6:1–3)?

c. What is one way you could honor your parents this week?

d. Ephesians 6:5–9 talks about the relationship between slaves and masters, but it can be applied to the boss-worker relationship. What do these verses teach you about working at your job? (If you are still in school, consider school your job.)

3. Get a close-up. Zoom in on one thing you discovered today.

4. Write Psalm 40:8 from memory.

Meaningful Makeover

Jesus said, "If anyone would come after Me, let him deny himself and take up his cross daily and follow Me" (Luke 9:23). Think back on all you have learned this week. Ask God if there is an area of your life where He wants you to let go. Is there a part of your life to which you have been holding tightly, but which you now see God wants you to let Him control? School? Career? Relationships?

Write a prayer below giving that part of your life to your loving and caring Father.

Remember to bring your uniform or other confidence-building outfit to your group's meeting.

Fashion
Finesse

A few words about finding the right clothes, building a
wardrobe, and looking your best

The Power of Fashion

You have power. You may not see yourself as powerful—but it's true. As women, we have power, and part of that power is in the clothes we choose to wear.

This doesn't mean that we have a special suit like Iron Man that gives us superpowers. We don't have a Superman cape. But all of the clothes we put on our bodies have a not-so-secret power over men's brains.

We can use this power for good or for bad.

A few years ago, a study was done at Princeton University in which the brains of male students were observed as they were shown pictures of women in different clothing. Brain scans revealed that when men saw pictures of scantily clad women, the part of the brain associated with tools—like hammers and drills—lit up. At the same time, some men showed no activity at all in the area of the brain where we think about another person's thoughts and feelings. Researchers were shocked because this area of the brain almost never shuts down.

Experts realized that when men saw women in very little clothing, they viewed them not as people to connect with, but as objects to be used. Wearing a bikini gives a woman power—the power to short-circuit a man's brain and shut down his ability to see her as a person.[3]

This is not the kind of power we want. We want the power to communicate with guys as equals. We desire the power to be valued for who we are and not just what we look like. We want power in the form of respect.

So let's use the power of fashion for good.

Now, I'm not saying that men do not have to take responsibility for their actions. I'm not trying to tell you that women are to blame for men's bad behavior. But it does mean that if we recognize that we have this kind of power, we can use it to get the kind of attention that we really want. We can use the power to be valued as persons and not merely as things to be used. We can use the power to help our brothers in Christ keep their thoughts pure.

Jason Evert, a Christian author who writes on the topic of modesty, says: "Women. Modesty means you have beauty and power. And you use that to teach men how to love you for the right reasons."[4]

You may think that the only way to get a guy to notice you is through how you look. It's true that he may indeed notice what you're wearing, but he will pay more attention to your outer beauty instead of your inner beauty. Guys are more likely to get to know the real you when you realize the power of modesty. Although you may catch the eyes of fewer men, you are more likely to capture the heart of the kind of guy you want to spend time with. Modesty increases the odds of finding someone who loves you for who you are and not for what you can give him.

Girls, let's realize the power of fashion. Be aware of how the clothes you wear or don't wear affect the men around you (especially their brains!). Choose to dress in a way that expects respect. Use your beauty and modesty to attract guys to the real you.

WEEK THREE

Bag the Handbag of Worry and Carry an Attitude of Trust

Memory Verse

[Cast] all your anxieties on Him, because He cares for you. 1 Peter 5:7

Day One

<><><><><><><><><><><><><><><><><><><><><><><><>

How Heavy Is Your Purse?

Anxiety in a man's heart weighs him down.
Proverbs 12:25

A bathroom scale was sitting in the middle of the room. As we entered the room for a party, my friends and I all murmured, "You've got to be kidding!" "You're not getting *me* on that thing."

It turned out the scale was there for a contest for the heaviest purse. One by one, we brought our bags to the scale to be weighed. Some of the purses were little bitty wallet-on-a-string styles. Some were cross-body messenger bags. Some were massive shoulder bags.

My friend Sophie won the prize with a purse that came in at just under ten pounds. No one was surprised. Sophie was famous for her humongous purse. We often teased her about her backbreaking bag—but guess who we turned to when we needed a bandage, toothpick, sewing kit, tape measure, hand sanitizer, cough drop, or aspirin?

Worry can be like that heavy purse. We don't mean to, but every day, we pick up that bag and put more worries in it. Maybe the day starts out fine, but then the algebra teacher announces a pop quiz, and you put "What if I fail this quiz?" into your worry bag. You pass a good friend in the hall, but she ignores you, and you stuff in the nagging question "What if she's mad at me?" Signs are posted for the prom, and into the bag goes "What if I don't get asked to the dance? What if I *never* get a date?"

What are you worried about? Not fitting in? Living up to your parents' expectations? Grades? Family difficulties? Relationships with the opposite sex? SAT scores? Finding a great job? That great big zit on your nose?

You might think you are the only young woman who has those worries. Everyone else looks so cool. Their lives look perfect. What could they possibly be concerned about?

You are not alone. A Canadian study revealed that three out of every four high school students surveyed admitted that they're worried about the future. More than half confessed that they lose sleep because they're worrying. Almost one in three said they felt like crying.[5]

God knows that sometimes you worry. He knows all of your *What if . . . ?* thoughts can be like my friend Sophie's purse strapped to your soul. Proverbs 12:25 says, "Anxiety in a man's heart weighs him down."

The good news is that God doesn't want you to continue to carry that huge bag of worries. He wants to carry it for you. Our memory verse this week is:

> [Cast all] your anxieties on Him, because He cares for you.
> 1 Peter 5:7

I know. That's kind of churchy language. But what God is telling you in this verse is this: "Don't keep carrying that huge bag of worries. Give Me everything that ties your brain in knots. Hand over all the problems that keep you up at night. Because I love you! Really. I want you to have the best life possible, a life of faith and confidence in Jesus. So trust Me. Give Me that super-size bag of problems."

I want you to try a little exercise to help you picture giving your worries to God. Get a few pieces of paper and a pen. On each piece of paper, write down one of the things you are worried about right now, like the chemistry test on Friday, the job interview next week, or the party planned for Saturday. If there isn't something specific that you are concerned about right now, write down the things that keep you up at night, like relationships with friends, family problems, or the future.

Now find a purse you're not using right now. (If you don't have an extra purse, use a box.) One at a time, put each piece of paper into the purse or box. As you slide it in, talk to God about the problem. Tell Him exactly how you feel. Admit your fears and doubts. Every one of them!

Once you have put all of your concerns into the purse or box, put it aside. Set it on a shelf or on the floor where it is out of the way but where you can still see it. As your fingers release their grip, tell God that you are handing over your worries to Him. Let Him know that you are letting go—and that you are trusting Him to take care of everything.

Next, write the words of 1 Peter 5:7 on a piece of paper: "[Cast] all your anxieties on Him, because He cares for you." Put this piece of paper in the purse or backpack you carry every day (or put it in your pocket). That way, when you open your purse or backpack or reach into your pocket, you will be reminded that God is handling your problems.

During the next few days, whenever you are tempted to pick up your worries again, look at the bag. Remind yourself that you have given all those problems to your heavenly Father, the all-powerful God who is more than able to take care of them. Mentally set that heavy bag down again.

Reread the verse in your purse. Remember: *God cares for you.*

> *Father, I admit it. I sometimes worry. Life sometimes seems overwhelming. What a relief to know that You are there to carry my worries for me. I give all my problems to You. I'm trusting You to take care of them. In Jesus' name. Amen.*

What Do I Worry About?

School, sports, how people see me, having time for my family and friends.
Torry

What is the average weight of a woman's handbag?

a. 3 pounds

b. 5 pounds

c. 21 pounds

(Answer: a. 3 pounds.)

Day One
◇◇◇◇◇◇◇◇◇◇◇◇◇◇◇◇◇◇◇◇◇◇◇◇◇
Wardrobe Workout

1. What kind of purse do you use? A mini-wallet on a string? A giant designer bag? Why do you like this kind of purse? In what way can a large purse remind us about God's care for us too? (If you are doing this study in a group, bring your favorite purse to the meeting for show-and-tell.)

2. Do the exercise we talked about in today's lesson. How did you feel after you gave God your worries?

3. In Matthew 6:25–34, Jesus teaches us what to do with our concerns. Read this passage and answer the following questions.

   a. What are some of the things Jesus tells us not to worry about (vv. 25–27)?

   b. Some people must live in a dangerous place or don't have enough food or clean water. What can such things teach us about worry?

   c. In verse 33, Jesus says that instead of worrying, we should "seek first the kingdom of God." What do *you* think it means to seek God's kingdom?

d. What is another way to deal with worry according to verse 34?

4. Get a close-up. Zoom in on one thing you discovered today.

5. Our memory verse for this week is 1 Peter 5:7: "[Cast] all your anxieties on Him, because He cares for you." To help you memorize this passage, write it on a 3 x 5 card or sticky note and carry it in your purse or backpack this week. Also write it out in the space below.

Day Two
◇◇◇◇◇◇◇◇◇◇◇◇◇◇◇◇
Miracle White

*[Cast] all your anxieties on Him, because He cares
for you. 1 Peter 5:7*

The bus died in the middle of the Mojave Desert. It made one last *ker-chunk* and then totally bit the dust.

I was on that bus with sixteen other musicians; we were in a Christian group named Joy, Inc., and we were touring the country. Every morning we woke up; repacked our suitcases; got on the bus; traveled to a new town; unloaded our keyboards, guitars, drums, and amps; set up in a new church; gave a concert; and put our equipment back on the bus. Each night we slept in a different bed, usually provided by a member of the church where we were performing. The next morning we started the whole process over again. The whole experience was exciting, exhilarating . . . and exhausting.

When I started that journey, I never suspected that there would be problems. Naïve, I know. But I figured we were all Christians. So we would always get along. And nothing would ever go wrong. The whole year was going to be a blast. Right?

Wrong. Have you ever tried living with sixteen other people on a school bus for a year? Sure, we had a lot of fun. But we also got on each other's nerves. We occasionally disagreed. Sometimes we were just plain sick of seeing each other's faces. It was then that I had to learn to depend on God instead of people.

But the best teacher I had in learning trust was not another person. The most effective teacher I had when God was teaching me to quit worrying and start trusting Him was . . . the bus.

The bus we traveled in was a converted school bus called Miracle White—so named because it was painted white and it was a miracle that it was even running. The fact that we were traveling in a school bus probably should have had me worrying from the beginning. I mean, school buses are designed to carry kids across town, not across the country.

But, hey, I was only eighteen. I didn't know anything about cars, let alone buses. So I just got on Miracle White with the others in the group and went where it took us without considering any potential problems.

Until March.

One weekend of that month, our group sang at a retreat at Lake Arrowhead in the mountains of California. We had a great time, but on the way down the mountain, we noticed a little something wrong with Miracle White—the brakes were on fire! Miracle White ended up in the repair shop, and we had to borrow a couple of vans to get ourselves and our equipment to our singing engagements in the area.

When the repair took longer than expected, we ended up canceling one singing engagement and then taking an all-night, twenty-four-hour drive from Los Angeles to Colorado for our next concert. Now that I knew there could be problems—that brakes could actually catch fire—I was worried. We had to drive over the mountains again. Would the brakes hold?

Thankfully, there were no problems with the brakes as we drove over the mountains. But in the middle of the night, as we were driving through the Mojave Desert, Miracle White suddenly died. Gave that one last *ker-chunk* and came to an immediate stop. What now?

Eventually, a kind driver came by and gave Bill, our leader, a ride into the next town. Bill came back with a tow truck—which, by the way, was painted with the company's name: Death Valley Towing. I was not terribly encouraged.

The next day, after spending a very short night in a bug-infested hotel, we found out that Miracle White's brakes were fine, but the engine had thrown a rod. It would need rebuilding. It would need parts shipped from Phoenix. It would need at least a week of repair time.

If I had been a little worried when the brakes were questionable, I was now upset and anxious. What were we going to do? How would we get the bus fixed? How would we get to our concerts?

That's when God taught me the truth of 1 Peter 5:7, "[Cast] all your anxieties on Him, because He cares for you."

God is serious when He tells us to give Him all of our concerns. He says, "Listen, I love you. I'm watching out for you. Let Me take care of your worries." And let me tell you, I was worried about our situation. We all were.

But that's where knowing God helps. As it turns out, knowing Him doesn't mean we won't have problems. But it does mean that when problems come, we know where to take them. Our little group came together and prayed. We brought our big bag of problems and threw them into God's lap, watching to see what He was going to do with them, and trusting that He would provide for us.

Miracle White did not live up to its name. But God lived up to His name of Provider in working out the details for us. After that horrible night in the roach-infested hotel, a local church offered to let us sleep on the floor of their building for a couple of nights. We also contacted some people from Las Vegas we had met at the Lake Arrowhead retreat. They generously offered to come get us and let us stay with them and other members of their church until the bus was fixed.

After two long weeks, Miracle White finally got back on its wheels. That experience changed me from a carefree teenager to a more wary adult. But it also proved to me that I don't have to deal with my worries alone. God wants to carry them for me.

Heavenly Father, thank You that You care for me. This life isn't perfect, and sometimes when things aren't going great, I worry. Help me to remember that You are always there to take my worries. You are more than willing to take care of all the details. Help me to trust You. In Jesus' name. Amen.

The thing that helps me is knowing that God will use everything that happens for my ultimate good. That's what I keep telling myself.
Kristin

Pray and let God worry.
Martin Luther

Day Two
<><><><><><><><><><><><><><><><><><><>
Wardrobe Workout

1. Have you had an experience that changed you from a carefree kid to a more cautious and careful person? Describe what happened.

2. Today, we talked about trusting in God's care when we are tempted to worry. Psalm 16 is a beautiful prayer that talks about God's care. Read the psalm and answer the questions below.

   a. Throughout the psalm, David talks about God's care. List some of the ways God takes care of us. (For instance, v. 7 tells us that God gives us "counsel," or instruction.)

   b. Which of the things you listed above mean the most to you today? (For example: I'm thankful for God's instruction, v. 7.)

   c. Write a short prayer thanking God for what you wrote in answer to the previous question.

3. Get a close-up. Zoom in on one thing you discovered today.

4. Write out our memory verse for this week: "[Cast] all your anxieties on Him, because He cares for you" (1 Peter 5:7). Read a phrase, then cover it and write it. Try to write as much of the verse as you can without looking.

Day Three
◇◇◇◇◇◇◇◇◇◇◇◇◇◇◇◇
Made Known

*Do not be anxious about anything, but in everything
by prayer and supplication with thanksgiving let your
requests be made known to God. And the peace of God,
which surpasses all understanding, will guard your hearts
and your minds in Christ Jesus. Philippians 4:6–7*

In college I had a mentor, Cheryl. We were both involved in the same organization—Campus Crusade for Christ. Every month, Cheryl and I met for lunch. She would ask me how things were going, and I would tell her about my goals, my dreams, and my struggles. She would listen patiently, pray with me, and help me brainstorm specific ways I could tame my troubles.

I wonder if Cheryl knows what a big help she was in my life. Simply having another Christian to confide in was huge. Sometimes I truly felt like I was the only person on campus who believed God existed. Being able to talk to another Christian was like finding water in the desert.

It was also a relief to be able to talk to someone about my problems. I found I was often keeping them bottled up. When life shook the bottle, my worries bubbled up in my brain like Diet Coke on Mentos. Spilling out my concerns to Cheryl released the pressure in my crowded head.

It is important to know how to deal with our worries. Popular media often shows unhealthy examples of dealing with our problems. Girls worried about their weight develop eating disorders to get to a certain size. Teens concerned about fitting in start drinking or experimenting with drugs to feel a part of things. Young women aching for acceptance give away their purity to someone who promises to love them but has no intention of keeping his word.

One of the best things you can do with your worries is talk about them. Sometimes simply getting them out into the open helps you realize that things aren't as bad as they seem. Often you will find that others have the same struggles.

I urge you to build a support team. Don't choose your friends on the basis of their popularity. Find friends who share your values and prove their loyalty to you. Don't be afraid to talk to your parents. They were teenagers once too. Although it's been awhile, they can still remember the challenges they faced and can sympathize with you about yours. Remember that your school counselor, pastor, and church youth leader are also available to listen to your fears. Seek out Christian advisors who can guide you to true answers to your problems.

Most important, talk about your worries with the One who loves you most of all. Philippians 4:6–7 says:

> Do not be anxious about anything, but in everything by
> prayer and supplication with thanksgiving let your requests
> be made known to God. And the peace of God, which
> surpasses all understanding, will guard your hearts and your
> minds in Christ Jesus.

God is asking us to open up to Him. He wants us to talk to Him about the things that make our minds spin. He wants us to be honest about the questions that keep us up at night. He truly wants to hear what's on our hearts.

The passage in Philippians tells us to pray about *everything*. Nothing is too big for God to handle. Nothing is too small. Nothing is too embarrassing.

I have to be honest about something: I tend to try to handle my problems by myself before I bring them to God. I work hard. If nothing happens, I work harder. Finally, when I discover I can't solve the puzzle on my own, I bring it to God. He probably shakes His head and smiles, knowing my life would have been so much easier if I had come to Him in the first place. Trying to solve the problem on my own instead of relying on God is a little like trying to make a smoothie with a knife and spoon instead of using a high-speed blender.

Look at the phrase "let your requests be made known to God." If Paul, the author of Philippians, were writing the same words in today's English, he would say something like "Keep on bringing your needs to God and never stop telling Him what you want." This is good news for you girls who love to talk. God never tires of hearing your voice. He wants to hear about all of your problems. So every time a concern pops into your head, turn it into a prayer. Change every little worry into a conversation with God.

God wants you to know that He is available to listen to your doubts and fears, your hopes and dreams. Keep on bringing your needs to God; He promises to hear every word.

Father, I know that I can talk to You about anything. Thank You that You care about the big things, the little things, and everything in between. Please also give me true friends and counselors who will listen to my worries and guide me in Your way. In Jesus' name. Amen.

I'm worried about school. I went to a private school before, and now I'm going to a big public school. I'm worried that I'm not going to know anybody or make new friends.

Kaitlyn

Build a Support Team

To whom can you go when you're worried? Who will give you a listening ear and good advice? Are any of these people on your support team?

• Trusted friends

• Parents

• Pastor

• Youth leader

• Teacher

• Counselor

Day Three
◇◇◇◇◇◇◇◇◇◇◇◇◇◇◇◇◇◇◇◇◇◇
Wardrobe Workout

1. Describe what happens to you when you hold your worries inside.

2. Who is on your team? List the people you know you could go to if you wanted to talk about your worries.

3. What do these passages tell us about God?

   a. Psalm 5:1–3

   b. Psalm 17:6

   c. Psalm 28:6–7

   d. Psalm 34:17–18

4. Get a close-up. Zoom in on one thing you discovered today.

5. Write out this week's memory verse. Try to do it without looking back at the words.

Day Four

◇◇◇◇◇◇◇◇◇◇◇◇◇◇◇◇◇

Say Thank You

*Do not be anxious about anything, but in everything
by prayer and supplication with thanksgiving let your
requests be made known to God. And the peace of God,
which surpasses all understanding, will guard your hearts
and your minds in Christ Jesus. Philippians 4:6–7*

"What do you say, dear?"

"Did you remember to say thank you?"

"Have you written your thank-you notes yet?"

How many times have you heard these words come out of your mom's mouth? Well, it turns out our mothers are right. It is a good thing to give thanks.

Even when we're worried.

It seems all wrong to be thankful when things aren't going right. How can I be grateful when my mind is spinning with problems?

But God says it right there in Philippians 4:6:

> Do not be anxious about anything, but in everything by
> prayer and supplication with *thanksgiving* let your requests
> be made known to God (emphasis added).

God invites us to bring all of our worries to Him and set them in His lap. But He wants us to do it with thanksgiving. He wants us to remember to say "Thank You."

This seems all backward. But even when your life is the pits, God wants you to look around and find something to be grateful for. Maybe you're worried about making friends at a new school—but you can still thank God for the cell phone that lets you keep in touch with your old friends. Perhaps your family is having some money problems—but you have parents who love you. Perhaps there's a big test on Friday—but hey, there are double-chocolate brownies for dessert tonight.

And most of all, even when you're having a terrible, horrible, no good, very bad day, you can thank Him that through Jesus you will have a fabulous, fantastic, amazing, very wonderful eternity. Thank Him that because of Christ's sacrifice on the cross you are forgiven. Thank Him that you are a part of His family.

God isn't demanding a thank-You note out of some kind of power trip. He knows that when we find something to be thankful for, it will refocus our life lenses. Instead of staring at our problems, we look at the blessings, and life won't seem so bad.

Gratitude also grows our faith. Every prayer of thanks for something good in our lives waters the tiny plant of trust growing in our hearts. We remember how God has answered our prayers before, and we believe He will come through again.

And when it seems like God is taking His sweet time in fixing our worries, thanksgiving builds up the trust that helps us to wait for God's answer. It helps us to accept what is.

Life is not perfect. But tough times can make us stronger. We can learn new life lessons. We can develop compassion for others who are facing similar problems. Most of all, those tough times can draw us closer to God. I don't know about you, but I usually spend a lot more time praying when life is tough than when everything is going according to plan. Looking back at difficult times, we can even thank God for the very things that made us worry, because we put our faith in Him and because we can trust that He will bring good out of everything.

So how do we do this? What are some practical ways to say "Thank You, God," even when our minds are tangled webs of worries?

- Try a gratitude journal. Use a notebook or pretty journal to record the little things in life that bring you joy.
- Keep a list of your favorite blessings in your purse. What are you most grateful for? Your mom? Your friends? Write them all down. When you're tempted to worry, pull out the list and say a little prayer of thanks.
- Write Philippians 4:6–7 and other verses about thankfulness on sticky notes and post them around your room or house. (Try Psalm 30:11–12; 75:1; and 107:1.)

- Write down all of your spiritual blessings. If you have faith in Jesus as your Savior, then you know that He offers you forgiveness for your sins, life in heaven forever, and the awesome privilege of a friendship with God. These blessings will never go away.
- Don't forget about all the little things that make life better. Every night, I thank God for my mattress (I love to sleep!). I'm grateful for my microwave (a cup of tea in two minutes!).
- Thank God for your blessings by helping others who may have bigger struggles than your own. Try volunteering at a hospital or homeless shelter. Sometimes this helps to put your own worries into perspective.

Thanksgiving changes us. Even when we're worried. Especially when we're worried. Our heavenly Father wants us to come to Him with our problems, but even before He has fixed them, He knows we'll be transformed by gratitude.

Father, things are not great right now. But I thank You. I thank You for all the little things in life that make me smile. I thank You that You are able to fix all the messes in my life. I thank You for Your presence here with me in the middle of it all. Amen.

Gratitude Gives Back

Gratitude not only loosens our grip on our worries; it helps us in a ton of other ways. Research shows that people who practice being thankful

- have fewer illnesses;

- have greater joy and enthusiasm for life;

- feel more loving and forgiving;

- have more energy; and

- cope better with stress.[7]

Day Four

Wardrobe Workout

1. What do you think? How can being thankful change your attitude?

2. Try one of the practical ways to say "Thank You, God" on pages 78–79. Did it help to change your worried mind? Why or why not?

3. The following verses talk about thanksgiving. Beside each reference, write why we can give God thanks.

   a. Psalm 30:11–12

   b. Psalm 75:1

   c. Psalm 107:1

4. Get a close-up. Zoom in on one thing you discovered today.

5. Write out this week's memory verse. No peeking!

Study Styles

God promises that when we give Him our problems, He will give us peace. One way to study the Bible is to look for PEACE: a **P**romise, an **E**xample to follow (or not to follow), an **A**ttitude we should have, a **C**ommand to obey, and an **E**nlargement of our view of God. Here is an example from John 14:

Promise: "Peace I leave with you; My peace I give to you" (v. 27).

Example: "Thomas said to Him, 'Lord, we do not know where You are going. How can we know the way?'" (v. 5). We can follow Thomas's example of asking questions.

Attitude: "Whoever has My commandments and keeps them, he it is who loves Me" (v. 21). This shows an attitude of obedience in love.

Command: "Let not your hearts be troubled. Believe in God; believe also in Me" (v. 1). This is a command to not worry, but believe.

Enlargement: (Here you will look for a verse that tells you something about God—who He is or what He does.) "But the Helper, the Holy Spirit, whom the Father will send in My name, He will teach you all things and bring to your remembrance all that I have said to you" (v. 26). The Holy Spirit teaches us and helps us remember all that Jesus said.

Now it's your turn. Find PEACE in Philippians 4:4–9.

Promise:

Example:

Attitude:

Command:

Enlargement:

Day Five
◇◇◇◇◇◇◇◇◇◇◇◇
In Training

Finally, brothers, whatever is true, whatever is honorable,
whatever is just, whatever is pure, whatever is lovely, what-
ever is commendable, if there is any excellence, if there
is anything worthy of praise, think about these things.
Philippians 4:8

"I'm telling you, Brian, come back here now!" I yelled at the five-year-old barreling down the sidewalk on his tricycle, who obviously had no intention of coming back.

This was one of my first babysitting jobs, and Brian was proving to be a handful. As soon as his mother's car pulled out of the driveway, Brian raced down the stairs of their second-floor apartment. He jumped on his fire engine–red tricycle and pedaled as fast as his little legs could spin.

I called and called for him to come back, but he acted as if he couldn't hear me. I started running after him.

I thought everything would be okay when he stopped at the end of the block. But just as I got near him, he turned the corner and took off again. Now I was wishing I had joined the track team. I could barely keep up with this kid.

When we had made it all the way around the block, Brian pulled into his driveway and got off the trike. I immediately put it in the garage, thinking that would solve the problem. But when I turned back to ask Brian what he wanted to do next, he was *running* down the sidewalk. I was on to his game now. He wanted me to follow him. Once again, he ran to the end of the block, where he turned around and watched for me. I followed at a leisurely pace. When I got within nabbing range, the five-year-old legs flew around the corner, and I was on the run again.

I thought that once again, Brian would go around the block, and then we would head back home. But we were near the park where the county fair was being held, and suddenly Brian took off toward the entrance gates to the fair. Now I had to sprint. Before I could catch him, Brian had run past the ticket takers, into the crowd. I didn't have any money with me, and it didn't matter. I needed to grab Brian *now* before I lost him in the crowd. I yelled, "Stop that kid!" One of the ticket takers grabbed him and handed him over to me.

I ended up carrying a wailing, flailing five-year-old six blocks back to his house while he was trying to stuff his hand in my mouth and pull out my hair. When we finally got back, I announced that we were going back upstairs and staying there. "If you come up without any fuss," I said, "I'll get you one of those popsicles your mom said you could have."

I began walking up the stairs. Brian was following me. *Good,* I thought. *Maybe the rest of the evening won't be such a nightmare.*

Just then, I felt something wet on my backside. Brian was *spitting* on me!

I lost it. I turned around and gave his rear end a little smack.

Brian looked up at me and said, "My mommy never does that."

That fact was all too obvious.

Why did I tell you this story? Obviously, I am not giving you tips on babysitting. I'm not sure what would have been the right way to handle Brian, but it was not my place to give even a little whack.

I'm letting you know about my babysitting disaster because that five-year-old terror on wheels reminds me of my thoughts. Sometimes my worries seem to be running down the sidewalk of my mind. Just when I think I can stop them and make them behave themselves, they take off again. How can I keep those worries under control?

Just as Brian the Brat clearly needed some discipline, our thoughts need training. Philippians 4:8 gives us a little coaching on how to think:

> Finally, brothers, whatever is true, whatever is honorable, whatever is just, whatever is pure, whatever is lovely, whatever is commendable, if there is any excellence, if there is anything worthy of praise, think about these things.

Maybe you've noticed that it doesn't work to simply tell yourself not to worry. Instead, we need to retrain our brains to think about something else. The verse in Philippians gives us our training program: Think about what is true, honorable, just, pure, lovely, excellent, and worthy of praise.

Let me give you an example of how I use this verse to retrain my mind. Right now, my daughter is living in China, working as a missionary. And yes, there are days that I worry about her. I'm concerned about her safety and health. I'm nervous for her as she adjusts to living in a foreign culture.

But it doesn't do any good for me to worry. So I first turn all those little concerns into prayers. I remember to thank God for keeping her safe so far. And then I use the Philippians 4:8 training program. I try to concentrate on what is true—God is in control and will take care of Anna. I tell myself to think about what is excellent—Anna's desire to serve God. I focus on what is worthy of praise—her dedication.

When your worries are acting like out-of-control preschoolers, use the Philippians 4:8 training program to get them to behave. Think about what is true and lovely in your life. Concentrate on what is good and pure. God promises His peace when we focus on Him.

Jesus, sometimes worries seem to run out of control in my mind. I know that You can help me train my thoughts. When I start to worry, help me to think about what is true and right, pure and lovely. In Your name. Amen.

Top Five Ways to Stop Worrying (Not!)

1. Think about your problem every waking moment.

2. Talk about it all the time.

3. Play the "What if . . . ?" game.

4. Imagine the worst-case scenario.

5. Never talk to God about the problem.

Day Five

∞∞∞∞∞∞∞∞∞∞∞∞∞∞∞∞∞∞∞∞∞∞∞

Wardrobe Workout

1. How have your thoughts been behaving lately? Check the name that is most like the activity in your brain in the last week.

   _____Angie the Angel

   _____Caitlyn the Calm

   _____Francis the Frantic

   _____Brian the Brat

2. Read Psalm 139:23.

   a. What does David ask God to do?

   b. What feelings (positive and negative) do you have when you realize God knows your thoughts?

3. Get a close-up. Zoom in on one thing you discovered today.

4. Write 1 Peter 5:7 from memory.

Meaningful Makeover

What problem in your life seems most like the out-of-control Brian the Brat? See if you can use the Philippians 4:8 training program to tame your thoughts. What about that problem is

true? _____

_____

honorable? _____

_____

just? _____

_____

pure? _____

_____

lovely? _____

_____

excellent? _____

_____

deserving praise? _____

_____

(If you can't find these qualities in that particular situation, look for them in other areas of your life.)

Don't forget to bring your favorite bag to your group's meeting!

Fashion Finesse

A few words about finding the right clothes, building a wardrobe, and looking your best

Beautiful Bags

A handbag is not only a way to carry around your daily essentials; it is a fun fashion accessory. The purse you choose can help you manage any little emergencies you may have and get through your day with style. Here are a few tips in picking the right bag for your look and personality.

Size: Fashion experts advise matching the size of the bag to the size of your body. Smaller bags for smaller people. Larger bags for larger people.

Shape: To look your best, choose a bag that is opposite your shape. The best purse shape for a tall, thin girl would be a round purse. A long, thin purse would work best for a short person.

Color: Look for a color that goes with most of your outfits. Black and brown are always classics, but red or turquoise can also coordinate with a lot of other colors.

Inside the purse: Some bags have a gazillion pockets, and some are just one big sack. Choose the one that suits your organizing personality. Do you like to keep everything neatly stowed where you can easily find it? Get one with lots of pockets. Do you think putting things back in a certain spot is a waste of time? Go with the big sack style.

Cost: What you spend may depend on how often you like to change purses. Do you like to have different purses for different outfits and occasions? It may be better to look for bargains. After all, the cheaper the price, the more bags you can buy! On the other hand, if you think changing bags is a hassle, you might consider finding a quality bag that will last, even if you have to spend a little more.

What kind of bag do you carry?

Purse Essentials

What do you carry in your purse? Here's a list of essentials and a few nice-to-have items. Put a checkmark next to the ones you carry. Circle the ones you want to add to your bag.

Essentials

___driver's license or ID

___cell phone

___keys

___a little cash for emergencies

Nice to Have

___a couple of aspirin

___lip gloss

___pens

___tissues

___hand sanitizer

___feminine hygiene supplies

___mini hairbrush

___hair ties

___toothbrush and toothpaste

___mints

___lotion

___mini sewing kit and safety pins

___stain remover (pen or towelette)

___Band-Aids

___sunglasses

___nail file

Can you think of any others?

WEEK FOUR

Pitch the Prom Dress of Pride and Wear Humility Instead

Memory Verse

Clothe yourselves, all of you, with humility
toward one another, for "God opposes
the proud but gives grace to the humble."
1 Peter 5:5

Day One
The Prom Dress of Pride

Clothe yourselves, all of you, with humility toward one another, for "God opposes the proud but gives grace to the humble." 1 Peter 5:5

The excitement is building. All eyes are on the fashion runway where tall, gorgeous models show off the latest styles. This event is billed as featuring "The Most Stunning Prom Dresses of the Season," and everyone present is anticipating the sight of party dresses and flowing gowns floating down the catwalk.

The curtain parts and out steps a beautiful model. Long, dark curls trail down her back. Her makeup is impeccable. She begins walking down the runway, carefully placing each perfect foot in front of the other. Her shoulders are back and her chin is lifted just so. Even before they notice the dress, everyone is thinking, *I want to be her.*

But of course, the dress is stunning. Red satin. One shoulder. Hugging all the right body parts before billowing out into an impossibly full skirt.

The announcer begins her description of the dress. The words barely register at first; everyone is mesmerized by the gown itself. But gradually, ears perk up—this is something *new.*

"We are pleased to debut this gown, the Prom Dress of Pride, from the Better-Than-You line. This brand-new label promises to show everyone you've got the look. No more trying to prove you are right—wear this dress and no one will doubt it. No more reaching out to others for attention—this gown guarantees to turn heads. Better hurry, ladies. This dress is going fast. Find it exclusively at MeMeAllMe.com."

* * * * * * *

Although we can't actually buy a gown from the Better-Than-You line, pride has been a trendy style since Eve's first fur outfit. Part of our nature feels the need to look good, be right, and appear better than others. We want people to admire us.

But the prom dress of pride has some disadvantages. Sure, at first people are drawn to someone who appears important, beautiful, or popular, but they soon drop away when they are constantly treated as lesser-thans. Wearing arrogance and the need to be right turns others away when they feel their opinions and viewpoints don't matter.

Think about it. What kind of person are you drawn to? The girl who looks down her perfectly shaped nose at you? The one who purposely avoids eye contact with you, lifting her chin ever so slightly as she passes you in the hall?

While you may wish those girls would reach out to you because they're in the popular crowd, the real friendships you have are probably with the girls whose faces light up when they see you. You can't wait to be with girls who treat you as an equal, or even as someone special. Your closest friends are those who are willing to share their own fears and even listen to yours.

Pride is a popular fashion. I know because I've tried to wear it. But I've found that it doesn't get me what I want. Pride keeps people at a distance. Pride leads to a lonely life.

But the worst consequence of pride is that it keeps me away from God. Remember how Cinderella couldn't go to the ball without a gown? The opposite is true in God's kingdom. The ball gown of pride prevents me from getting into the celebration of God's grace. With all those layers of superiority, I can't even get through the door of God's mercy. When I'm wearing the gown of arrogance, I don't see my desperate need for God's forgiveness. Pride pushes God away.

But when I ditch the fancy prom dress of pride, I discover that the God I have been pushing away is really a loving Father who has been standing there with His arms open, waiting to embrace me. When I admit that I need Him, He is more than ready to listen to me, answer my prayers, and be a part of my life.

That prom dress of pride? God asks us to ignore all the hype. The better-than-you line will not actually bring happiness.

Instead, God asks us to wear humility:

> Clothe yourselves, all of you, with humility toward one another, for "God opposes the proud but gives grace to the humble." 1 Peter 5:5

To get into God's kingdom, God doesn't demand an elegant gown. It's the Cinderella story in reverse—He wants us to wear the tattered dress of a servant. In fact, the word *clothe* in the passage from 1 Peter comes from a Greek word that refers to an apron that was worn by slaves in New Testament times. When we ask God, He will help us get rid of the I'm-better-than-you clothing and give us a dress of humility. This new gown will help us to see each person we meet as special in God's eyes. It will help us to get involved in people's lives, even when it might be messy or inconvenient.

In return, God promises His grace—His love, His forgiveness, and His strength. When we pitch the prom dress of pride, we gain true friends who don't care about a façade. We win a closer relationship with a God who infinitely cares for us.

Father, sometimes I think I need to wear a better-than-you attitude in order to go to the prom of life. But I realize that You want me to wear the gown of humility. Give me the clothing that will keep me close to You. Weave Your grace into my life so I can see others as You see them— with eyes of love. In Jesus' name. Amen.

Pricey Prom Quiz

Going to the prom or any formal affair can be expensive. The costs of the dress, shoes, tux, limo, and pre-dance activities can really add up. What do you think is the average amount spent on going to the prom in the United States? (See the answer below.)

a. $648

b. $1,139

c. $1,729

Do you think spending that much is worth it? Brainstorm with your friends on ways to keep costs down. How else might you use the money you save?

(Answer: b. $1,139 in 2013[8])

Day One
<><><><><><><><><><><><><><><><><><>
Wardrobe Workout

1. Do you have a prom dress or other formal in your closet? What does it look like? If you don't have one, describe the gown of your dreams. Bring your dress or a picture of your dream dress to your group's meeting.

2. Read the following statements and check whether you agree or disagree.

   The people I admire pay attention only to themselves.
   ___ Agree
   ___ Disagree

   The people I want as my friends don't know I'm alive.
   ___ Agree
   ___ Disagree

   The people I'm close to don't care what I think.
   ___ Agree
   ___ Disagree

   My closest friends pretend they're perfect.
   ___ Agree
   ___ Disagree

   Now describe the kind of person you want to be.

3. Read 1 Peter 5:5–7.

a. This passage talks about humility. Look up *humility* or *humble* in a dictionary and write the definition here.

b. Using that definition and what you learned today, how would you describe a humble person?

c. Verse 5 tells us one specific way we can show humility when we are young. What is that?

d. What does God promise to do for us when we humble ourselves (v. 6)?

4. Get a close-up. Zoom in on one thing you discovered today.

5. Our memory verse for this week is 1 Peter 5:5: "Clothe yourselves, all of you, with humility toward one another, for 'God opposes the proud but gives grace to the humble.'" To help you memorize this passage, print a photo of you in a formal dress, or find a picture of a prom dress you like. Write out 1 Peter 5:5 and post both the verse and the picture on your mirror. Also, write the verse in the space below.

Day Two

◇◇◇◇◇◇◇◇◇◇◇◇◇◇◇◇◇◇◇◇◇◇◇◇◇◇

The Impact of Humility

Pride goes before destruction, and a haughty spirit before
a fall. Proverbs 16:18

In sixth grade I took a spectacular fall because of a bit of pride.

The school I attended was part of a large church. During the school year, each class took turns singing for the church services. Well, when I was in sixth grade, our entire class was learning to play the recorder. And we were getting pretty good. One day, our teacher, Mr. Giese, announced that our class was going to perform for an evening service. Most of the class would sing, but three of us would be chosen to play the recorder part. I tried to play it cool when I was picked to be one of the three, but inside I was bursting with—I might as well say it—pride.

Before the church service that night, I changed into a dress and my first pair of panty hose! (Believe it or not, there was a time when panty hose were cool.) I was really going to wow everyone: new dress, recorder, *and* panty hose.

When I got to church, I climbed the stairs to the balcony with my recorder and I heard the organ music grow louder with each step. When I reached the balcony, I paused and looked down the short, steep flight of stairs to the front of the balcony where I was to go. Mr. Giese played the organ in front of me. Most of my classmates were already in the pews on either side of the aisle. *Good,* I thought. *I can make a grand entrance.*

I took a step. And another. Then disaster struck. Somehow, I tripped and landed on my bottom with a thud loud enough for Mr. Giese to hear above the organ music. Loud enough for him to stop playing and look to see what had happened. Loud enough for all the kids in my class to shake with quiet-as-possible laughter.

I looked down at my panty hose. Both knees had holes the size of dinner plates. A million runners scampered up each leg. My brand-new panty hose were no longer so impressive, and everybody had seen me fall.

My sixth-grade experience was a perfect example of Proverbs 16:18:

> Pride goes before destruction, and a haughty spirit before a
> fall.

While that encounter with pride led to a literal fall, there have been many more times when my better-than-you attitude has resulted in humiliating failure. What is it about pride that trips me up? I think it may cause me to fall because I'm looking down at other people rather than watching where I'm going. I'm too busy staring at myself to notice any potential dangers. I'm so worried about how I look that I forget to look around me.

In order to avoid the consequences of pride, I need to wear humility more often. Humility isn't a hot style today. You don't see too many celebrities wearing it. But it makes a unique fashion statement.

It's unique because almost everyone in the world is like me—they wear *pride*. When I'm wearing pride, I'm concerned about one person and one person only—me. But humility? Humility thinks about others.

Pride continually gazes at a mirror. Humility looks at the girl next to her.

Pride tries to focus all attention on herself. Humility asks her friend how *she* is doing.

Pride expects praise. Humility looks for ways to build up others.

Pride demands to be first. Humility pushes others to the front of the line.

Pride wonders what others think of her. Humility just thinks of others.

The night my panty hose–performance pride caused such an impressive fall, I snuck downstairs after the service to wait for my parents. While I was hiding behind a pillar to conceal my hideous legs, I overheard a man say to his wife on their way out of church, "Do you know what made that sonic boom before the service began?" That was not the kind of impact I had wanted to make; I tried to make myself invisible.

It's natural to want to impress everyone around us with our beauty, our intelligence, our skills. But the truth is, we will make a bigger impact on the world when we wear humility. Although it seems to go against all logic, in God's kingdom, pride is just a passing fad. Humility is a fashion that gets noticed, here on earth and in heaven.

Jesus, thank You for Your example of humility. You chose to be unnoticed when You could have commanded all the attention. Help me to make an impact on the world by being aware of others and putting their needs ahead of my own. Amen.

What Humility Looks Like

When I wonder what humility looks like, I think of Jesus.

- Instead of coming to earth as a rich and powerful king, Jesus came as a small baby born to a poor family.

- Instead of demanding worship and respect, He washed His disciples' smelly, dirty feet.

- Instead of pushing crowds of people away when He needed rest, Jesus fed them, taught them, and healed their hurts.

Day Two

Wardrobe Workout

1. Have you ever had a "pride goes before a fall" experience? Write about it here. Remember: sometimes our most embarrassing moments become our funniest stories!

2. Today, we talked about the difference between pride and humility. Using what you learned and recalling your own experiences, complete the following sentences:

   a. Pride is _____.

   b. Humility is _____.

3. Read the following verses and record the results of pride.

   a. Proverbs 11:2

   b. Proverbs 29:23

   c. Isaiah 2:17

4. Get a close-up. Zoom in on one thing you discovered today.

5. Write out our memory verse for this week: "Clothe yourselves, all of you, with humility toward one another, for 'God opposes the proud but gives grace to the humble'" (1 Peter 5:5). Read a phrase, then cover it and write it. Try to write as much of the verse as you can without looking.

Day Three

◇◇◇◇◇◇◇◇◇◇◇◇◇◇

The Spotlight

Let each one test his own work, and then his reason to
boast will be in himself alone and not in his neighbor.
Galatians 6:4

"Making our dreams come true . . ."

Under the bright lights of the West High auditorium, my two best friends belted out the words to the *Laverne & Shirley* theme song.

It was the annual pop concert. The school choirs sang a few numbers, but every choir member also had the chance to audition to sing a solo or duet. My friends, Deb and Barb, beat out a lot of competition with their version of the popular song "Making Our Dreams Come True." I had to admit they were terrific.

Until that point, Deb, Barb, and I had been inseparable throughout our senior year. Choir concerts. Football games. We did them all together. So when it was time for the pop concert, I was a little disappointed when the other two members of our trio decided to do a duet. They tried to include me by letting me come onstage with them to play the tambourine, but I felt they were simply throwing me a pity part. I felt Not. Good. Enough.

So I did what any teenager would do. I upstaged them.

Actually, I didn't step out on the stage intending to steal the show. I was simply going to go out there and add a little percussion to their song. But somehow, under the bright lights, I felt the sudden urge to swing my 1950s-style ponytail around and bang the tambourine on my swaying hips. I got a little carried away, and soon the audience was laughing at me instead of appreciating the fabulous singing.

My friends were not amused.

Once again, I got in trouble because of my old enemy—pride. The bad thing about pride is that it can't let someone be better. It doesn't allow anyone else to have the spotlight. Pride looks at others and asks, *"How can I outdo them? How can I turn all the attention toward me?"*

Pride brings us down when it plays the comparison game. When we feel the constant need to be better than someone else, we will always lose. Galatians 6:4 tells us:

> Let each one test his own work, and then his reason to
> boast will be in himself alone and not in his neighbor.

Did you catch that? This verse talks about a positive kind of pride. It tells me that I can take pride in myself. I can look at my own actions and decide: Did I do something good? Can I be pleased with my achievements? If so, I can be happy with my efforts.

But the negative side of pride messes me up when I not only try to be *good*, but *better*.

At that pop concert, I sang a solo. And it went pretty well. It should have been enough to feel a bit of satisfaction in my own part in the show without stealing the attention from my friends. My downfall was when I couldn't let them be better than me for the three and a half minutes of their song.

What's the difference between good pride and bad pride? Good pride can be defined as "A sense of one's own proper dignity or value; self-respect."[9] God created each of us in His image. He doesn't want us to walk around acting like we are worthless. We are important simply because we are daughters of the King.

Another definition of good pride is "Pleasure or satisfaction taken in an achievement."[10] You can be proud of the fourteen points you shot for your basketball team. You can feel good about your A in calculus. You can be pleased that you took the time to serve at the food pantry.

But there is also bad pride. This kind of pride can be defined as "Arrogant or disdainful conduct or treatment; haughtiness" or "an excessively high opinion of oneself; conceit."[11] This kind of pride loudly compares the fourteen points with a teammate's five. This kind of pride brags about the A in calculus. This kind of pride makes sure everyone knows about the work at the food pantry.

So let's not steal the show. Let's take our turn in the spotlight, but let's let others have their time onstage too. Let's feel a little pride in a job well done, but applaud when our friends are doing something great. Don't play the comparison game: be good, even great, but not better.

Father, I'm sorry for when I have felt the need to be the one in the spotlight. Help me to be proud but not conceited. Let me see that I'm important not because I'm better than someone else, but simply because I'm part of Your family. In Jesus' name. Amen.

Don't Steal the Show: Healthy Pride in Action

1. **Accept applause gracefully.** When someone gives you a compliment, simply say thank you. Don't make a big deal by going into detail about how you won the contest, got the part, and so forth. But don't put yourself down, either; it only makes you look like you are trying to get more compliments.

2. **Put others in the spotlight.** Use every opportunity you can to applaud your friends and build others up.

3. **Be willing to work backstage.** Once in a while, insist that others take the stage while you do the work that no one sees.

Day Three
Wardrobe Workout

1. Have you ever been upstaged? How did you feel when someone else had to top your story or tell everyone what he or she did was better?

2. We see good pride and bad pride in action almost every day. Think about how you or your acquaintances showed examples of each.

   a. Good pride:

   b. Bad pride:

3. Jesus could have stolen the show by coming to earth as a powerful king. Instead, He came as a helpless baby. Read Philippians 2:1–11 and answer these questions about Jesus' example of humility.

   a. How can we show humility according to verses 3 and 4?

   b. Verse 5 tells we should have the same attitude as Jesus. Look at verses 6–8 and write some phrases that demonstrate His humility. (Example: "He emptied Himself, by taking the form of a servant," v. 7.)

   c. Look at the phrases you just wrote. Ask God to show you which of those actions or attitudes He would like you to take this week. Write a short prayer here, asking Him to help you put it into action.

4. Get a close-up. Zoom in on one thing you discovered today.

5. Write out this week's memory verse. Try to do it without looking back at the words.

Day Four

◇◇◇◇◇◇◇◇◇◇◇◇◇◇◇◇◇◇◇◇◇◇◇◇◇◇◇◇◇◇

Base Your Pride on This

But God shows His love for us in that while we were still
sinners, Christ died for us. Romans 5:8

I stared at my first college report card. Most of the grades were As and Bs. Not bad.

But there was one grade that stuck out. Aural Music Theory: C.

Not good.

I had struggled with this class all semester long. The professor asked us to do a whole list of seemingly impossible tasks: "Listen as I play this chord on the piano, and identify its quality. Write down this rhythm as I tap it out. Listen to this melody and write it out note by note." I knew I wasn't getting an A in that class.

But a C . . . For someone who had always prided herself on good report cards, a C was depressing.

I was never good at athletics. In grade school, I was always the last kid picked for teams. I knew I would never win a beauty pageant; my sister got all the natural good looks in the family. So I based all my self-esteem on the fact that I was pretty good at memorizing facts and understanding algebra and taking tests.

What did it mean if I wasn't good at school anymore?

Most of us tend to base our identity on our looks, our skills, or our intellect. Maybe you've always been the Cute Girl. Or perhaps you could run fast from the time you were in first grade. Or like me, you were always the one who could ace a test.

The world notices your specialness in that area and rewards you with trophies or scholarships. Who you are is based on that recognition, and so you try a little harder and work a little longer, just to keep those rewards coming.

We take pride in who we are.

Now, it isn't necessarily wrong to find satisfaction in the gifts God has given us. He has blessed each of us with a unique set of talents to use for His glory. He wants us to train and practice and develop our gifts so we can help our fellow human beings on earth.

But the problem comes when we base our identity in those gifts. We run the risk of losing the ability to like ourselves when all of our self-esteem is wrapped up in being able to please certain people or perform certain tasks. Because what happens if we can't do them anymore?

God wants you to see that you are not just Beauty Queen, Athlete, or Comedian. You are His child, and He loves you not because you are pretty or smart. He loves you because He loves you.

Romans 5:8 says:

> But God shows His love for us in that while we were still
> sinners, Christ died for us.

It doesn't say, "God shows His love for you while you were beautiful." It doesn't say, "God shows His love for you while you were winning races." It does say, "God shows His love for us while we were still messed up." It does say, "Christ died for us when we didn't look like much."

God loves us. Period.

And that is where your identity and pride should be based. Your self-esteem won't be rocked as long as you keep in mind this one timeless truth: God loves you as you are.

I wish I could say that when I got that C on my college report card, my self-esteem didn't suffer because I simply reminded myself of God's unconditional love for me. Or that I have never struggled with this problem since then. The truth is, in this performance-based world, it will always be a challenge to remind ourselves that our value comes from the simple fact that we are loved by the Creator of the universe.

But it's a challenge worth accepting because when you get that bad grade on the report card, you will still know you are special. When you finish in last place, you are still valuable. When someone else gets noticed, you are still loved. When you know you sinned big, you are still forgiven because of the cross.

Remember, you are not only Gifted Athlete, Amazing Brainiac, Ordinary Girl, or even Sinner. You are Child of the King.

Father, there are days when I feel like a loser. I try so hard. Sometimes I get the recognition I crave and I feel good. But often I fail and I feel really bad about myself. Thank You that I don't have to perform for You. Thank You for loving me and forgiving me simply because Jesus died for me. Amen.

What If I Don't Feel Pretty or Talented?

Some of you might be thinking, "But I've never been pretty or athletic or smart. I wonder if I have any gifts at all!" Trust me—you do have talents. Perhaps you haven't discovered them yet, but God gives each of us a special role to fill. In the meantime, continue to find your specialness in the fact that you are a child of the King!

Day Four
Wardrobe Workout

1. Which of these roles give you a sense of self-worth? Check any you identify with.

   _____Brainiac

   _____Athlete

   _____Beauty Queen

   _____Class Comedian

   _____Caring Friend

   _____Helper

_____Musician

_____Actor

_____Domestic Diva

_____Artist

_____Other

2. Do you sometimes feel pressure to perform well in these roles in order to feel good about yourself? Why or why not?

3. Personalize the truth of today's Bible passage, Romans 5:8: "But God shows His love for us in that while we were still sinners, Christ died for us."

   a. In the blank below, write a recent disappointment or failure. For example: But God shows His love for me even when I get a C in Music Theory.

   But God shows His love for me even when _____
   _____.

   b. How does that truth make you feel?

4. Get a close-up. Zoom in on one thing you discovered today.

5. Write out the memory verse for this week.

Study Styles

A fascinating way to explore the Bible is to do a word study. You can learn a lot about a topic by choosing a specific word or subject and then finding verses in the Bible where the word is used. With digital and online Bibles, this is easier than ever. For instance, you could go to Biblegateway.com, click on Keyword Search, and type in your chosen word. This site will list all the verses that contain this word, and you can read them right on your computer screen or tablet.

Since we are studying pride and humility this week, try typing in one of those words. Choose five of your favorite verses from the search results, and write down what you learned about pride or humility. (If you don't want to do your own search, here are five of my favorite verses about humility: 2 Chronicles 7:14, Psalm 25:9, Psalm 149:4, Daniel 4:37, James 4:10.)

Verse   **What I Learned**

1._____   _____

                                        _____

                                        _____

2._____   _____

                                        _____

                                        _____

3._____   _____

                                        _____

                                        _____

4._____   _____

                                        _____

                                        _____

5._____   _____

                                        _____

                                        _____

Day Five

<><><><><><><><><><><><><><><><><><><>

Take the Job Anyway

Behold, I am the servant of the Lord; let it be to me
according to your word. Luke 1:38

A young woman sat by the window, sewing. As she watched her needle glide in and out of the fabric, she thought about the day she would wear this dress—her wedding day.

Suddenly, there was a flash of light, and an angel appeared before her. Well, at least she *thought* it was an angel—she had never seen one before.

Even before the young woman could take a breath or slow down her pounding heart, the angel spoke: "Hello. You are blessed by the Lord. He is with you."

The angel tried to calm the young woman's fears. "Don't be afraid. God has noticed you and has given you a special role in His plan. You will soon become pregnant and give birth to a son and call His name Jesus."

Now the young woman was not only afraid; she was very confused. "Um . . . not to contradict you," she said, "but I don't see how this is going to happen. See, I'm a virgin."

"The Holy Spirit will come upon you and the power of the almighty God will hover over you. Your child will be called the Son of God."

* * * * * *

Of course, this is the story of Mary, the mother of Jesus. She was probably about your age—or maybe even a little younger—when she had a surprise visit from an angel. The day Gabriel showed up probably began like any other day. Maybe Mary was sewing, or sweeping, or cooking dinner—when suddenly, life changed forever.

I wonder what went through Mary's head when she heard Gabriel's news. We'll never know, of course. But if I had been Mary and received that surprising news, maybe I would have thought, *God certainly made the right decision when He picked me! I'm clearly the best person for this important task.*

Or maybe the first thing that would have gone through my mind would be *Wow! How am I going to get out of this "special" job? I don't know too many people who will believe me when I tell them I got pregnant by God. This is not going to look good.*

Or perhaps what I would have told Gabriel was this: "Okay, Gabe. I'll go along with your plan if you will just go out there in the streets and announce to everyone that I, Mary, have been chosen to be the mother of the Savior."

But I wasn't there and Mary didn't say any of those things. Instead, she said, "I am the Lord's servant. May everything you have said come true."

Mary knew the questions that would come when people noticed she was pregnant. She realized that very few would believe her answers. She accepted the fact that humiliation would probably be a constant companion throughout the pregnancy and maybe for the rest of her life.

And still she declared herself the Lord's servant.

I don't know if I would have done the same. If I'm going to do a hard job, I want everyone to know. If I'm misunderstood, I want to clear everything up so all of my friends and family know I have done nothing wrong. I probably would have begged Gabriel to make a public announcement, send out a group email, and post selfies on Facebook and Instagram. I would want everyone to know that I was personally picked for the most important job a woman could have. I would make sure that everyone understood that I was the chosen one.

But Mary decided to serve in humility. She set aside her pride and willingly took a job that would lead to people whispering behind her back or shunning her in the marketplace. In effect, she told Gabriel, "I'll do anything God asks of me."

I ask myself, *Am I willing to do anything God asks of me?*

If I'm ready to pitch out that prom dress of pride, God may respond by asking me to serve in a new way. He might give me a job that isn't glamorous at all. He may ask me to help where it's messy or hard. And I might not get the pat on the back or the praise I think I deserve.

But if I follow Mary's example, I'll take the job anyway.

Father in heaven, You know that I sometimes try to avoid the jobs that won't be noticed, the work that's hard and messy. But I want to be like Mary and serve in humility. Help me to say, "I'll do anything You want, Lord." In Jesus' name. Amen.

Be like Mary

None of us will get Mary's job, but we can all have her willing attitude and humbly serve wherever we are needed, even in ways that may not get a lot of attention. Here are a few ideas:

• Do the dishes without being asked.

• Volunteer at a local hospital.

• Stay after a youth group meeting to help clean up.

• Befriend the person who is often ignored.

• Offer to babysit for free for a busy young mom.

• Mow a neighbor's grass.

• Sing at a nursing home.

• Visit an elderly neighbor.

• Volunteer to help a disabled student at school.

• Surprise your mom by cleaning the bathroom.

• Help a Sunday School teacher.

• Take a younger sibling or cousin out for ice cream.

Day Five

◇◇◇◇◇◇◇◇◇◇◇◇◇◇◇◇◇◇◇◇◇◇◇◇◇

Wardrobe Workout

1. Imagine you are Mary. What would have been your first reaction when Gabriel told you his news?

2. Read Mary's song of praise in Luke 1:46–55. This passage is often called "The Magnificat" because here Mary *magnifies*—glorifies—God.

   a. Verse 48 says that God noticed something about Mary. What did He notice?

   b. Why do you think that attitude was important for the job Mary was given?

   c. The last part of verse 48 reads, "For behold, from now on all generations will call me blessed." Do you think Mary is bragging here? Why or why not? (Reread verse 49 for added insight.)

d. Mary lists many things God has done (vv. 50–54). Write some of them here.

e. Which of those has God done for you lately?

3. Get a close-up. Zoom in on one thing you discovered today.

4. Write 1 Peter 5:5 from memory.

Meaningful Makeover

Read the "Be like Mary" sidebar on page 111. Do you have any more ideas for low-profile service? List them here.

Choose two service ideas that you would like to perform in the next week. Write them below. Come up with a plan for how and when you will carry out your service.

Service	Plan to accomplish the service
Example:	
Visit an elderly neighbor	Tomorrow after school I will bake cookies and take a plate of them to Mrs. Smith down the street.
1. _____	_____ _____ _____ _____
1. _____	_____ _____ _____ _____

Don't forget to bring your prom dress or picture of a favorite gown to your group's meeting!

Fashion Finesse

A few words about finding the right clothes, building a wardrobe, and looking your best.

Seven Tips for a Fabulous Formal

Whether you're going to prom, graduation, a formal dance, or shopping for a another special occasion, you want to look your best. Here are a few tips for finding the right look for a formal event.

Be dazzling. But not too much. Usually simple styles are best. Too many ruffles or sparkles, and people might see only the dress and not you. Let the true dazzle come from your smile.

Be comfortable. When buying your dress and shoes, make sure you do everything in them that you will be doing at the event. Walk, sit, bend over, try a few dance steps. If the shoes are pinching your toes or slipping off your heels after a few minutes, your feet will be screaming at the dance.

Be true to yourself. Even if it's not the very latest style, choose a dress that flatters your shape and coloring.

Be money-wise. Find your perfect dress at consignment shops, on clearance racks, or even in your sister's closet. Don't spend a fortune on a dress you may wear only once.

Be chic. Choose a simple, classic dress and then make it fabulous by adding trendy jewelry, shoes, and handbag to complete your look.

Be prepared. Practice your look the weekend before. Fix your hair, do your makeup, try on your dress and accessories. That way, you will know if you need to pick up some new eye shadow or one more hair clip.

Have a great time!

WEEK FIVE

Get Rid of Envy Green and Put on the Color of Contentment

Memory Verse

> I know how to be brought low, and I know how to abound. I have learned the secret of facing plenty and hunger, abundance and need. Philippians 4:12

Day One

◇◇◇◇◇◇◇◇◇◇◇◇

Envy Green

Surely vexation kills the fool, and jealousy slays the
simple. Job 5:2

What colors do you like to wear? Bright red? Basic black? Bubble gum pink?

Green happens to be one of my best colors. My closet has sage green sweaters, teal tops, and apple green tees. I love to wear them all.

However, there is another shade of green that I sometimes wear—envy green. Even though that shade of green doesn't look good on anyone, I still have days when I put it on and stubbornly refuse to take it off. At one point in my life, envy green was my everyday go-to color.

We had recently moved to the Chicago area and were living in an older home. I had always thought it would be fun to live in a quaint old house. Unfortunately, this home did not fit into that category. It had all the problems of a fifty-year-old building, but none of the charm.

I tried not to complain—I really did—but this old house left a lot to be desired. It had lots of windows, but most of them were painted shut. It had two bathrooms, but the upstairs bathroom had only two square feet of floor space. The kitchen came with a stove—but it was from the 1970s.

The basement was especially annoying. We were told that the man who had built the house had dug the basement out by hand, which means it was anything but level. Plus it leaked. Every time it rained, a puddle the size of Lake Michigan appeared at the bottom of the stairs. To get to the washer and dryer, I had to leap over the puddle with my laundry basket.

Speaking of laundry, what I hated most about the house was the water. Instead of city water, this house had its own well. At first I thought, *Well water—no problem*. I had grown up in a house with well water, and there was never any trouble. So we hooked up the washer and dryer, and I popped in a big load of whites. But when they came out of the washer, they were orange!

Apparently, there was a lot of iron in the water. This even affected my hair. I usually wash my hair in the shower, and after a short time of sudsing up in this water, I had an orange streak going down the back of my blond hair!

So here I was, living in the House That Turned Everything Orange, when a new subdivision started up about a mile away. These houses were luxury homes—three times the size of my house. I was sure that these mansions didn't have basements with wavy floors and lakes, or appliances from the seventies. Surely all the windows opened, and the water didn't turn the laundry a hideous orange. The differences between my home and those new homes were way too obvious to me, and my life took on a little green streak (to go with my orange hair).

Every day, I woke up, looked at my living conditions, and grabbed another envy-green outfit.

It wasn't the first time I wore that color. In high school, I was jealous of the girls who had the perfect shape or better hair. I envied those who got the solos in choir or were picked for homecoming court. I continually compared myself with those who had more friends, more money, more style, more talent.

But the trouble with envy is that it eats away our happiness. Jealousy devours our joy. The Bible tells us:

> Surely vexation kills the fool, and jealousy slays the simple.
> Job 5:2

Constantly looking at what others have and I don't is a certain joy killer. Every minute spent wishing for what someone else has takes another bite out of my happiness. Every second spent wondering how I can get my life to match up with others gobbles up my contentment.

Because whenever I'm looking at someone else's popularity, beauty, or wealth, I'm not noticing my own. I look right past the blessings God has given me.

Eventually I realized this while I was living in the House That Turned Everything Orange. Although this house was definitely not my dream home, I knew it was the house we could afford, so I tried to look for its good points. It was big enough for our small family. It was warm and cozy. Friends and family filled the house with laughter.

When I remembered the blessings of the house I did have, I discovered joy again. Wearing envy green every day had nibbled away at my happiness, but when I deliberately kept that color in my attitude closet, happiness reappeared. Lose the envy and choose joy.

Giver of all good gifts, it's so easy for me to focus on what I don't have. But when I do that, my joy disappears. Help me to consciously look at what You have already given me. Help me to choose joy. In Jesus' name. Amen.

Effects of Envy

Envy is a destructive emotion. It can harm us mentally and physically. A recent study showed that envious people are more likely to feel

• hostile,

• angry,

• anxious,

• irritable,

• depressed, and

• stressed.[12]

When you start to experience envy, remember that it does you more harm than good! Take your emotions to God and ask Him to help you find the good things in your life.

Day One
◇◇◇◇◇◇◇◇◇◇◇◇◇◇◇◇◇◇◇◇◇◇◇◇◇◇
Wardrobe Workout

1. Search your wardrobe for an item in a shade of green. Bring it to your group meeting. Compare your green garment with the others in your group. Which item do you like best? Do you agree that comparing yourself with others can lead to envy? Why or why not?

2. Turn to page 142 and read "Meaningful Makeover." This week we are going to keep a gratitude journal.

   Put an X on the line below that marks your level of contentment now, before writing in the gratitude journal.

●————————————————|————————————————●

I'm constantly comparing what   I'm satisfied with
I have with what others have.   what I have.

Write in the gratitude journal on page 142 every day this week.

3. Look up these passages about envy. What does the Bible say are the effects of this destructive emotion?

   a. Psalm 37:1, 7, 8

   b. Proverbs 14:30 (Note: "The bones" was an expression for the whole body.)

   c. James 3:16

4. Get a close-up. Zoom in on one thing you discovered today.

5. Our memory verse for this week is Philippians 4:12: "I know how to be brought low, and I know how to abound. In any and every circumstance, I have learned the secret of facing hunger and plenty, abundance and need." To help you memorize this passage, write it on a sticky note and post it in your locker, on your mirror, or on your computer. Also, write the verse in the space below.

Day Two

◇◇◇◇◇◇◇◇◇◇◇◇◇◇◇◇◇◇

Facebook Envy

But as for me, my feet had almost stumbled, my steps had
nearly slipped. For I was envious of the arrogant.
Psalm 73:2–3

More than seventeen solid days a year.

That's how much time the average young adult spends on social media.[13]

Websites like Facebook and Instagram and Snapchat are a great way to connect with friends, keep long-distance friendships going, and catch up on the latest happenings in our social circles.

But social media not only sends news over the Internet; sometimes it delivers envy.

A friend posts a picture of a new car she bought. *Hmm . . . wish I could afford that.*

A cute picture of a FB friend's puppy gets fifty-one likes. *Wow, my dog's picture only got twenty-three likes.*

Two friends both post about the time they spent together over the weekend. *Wonder why I wasn't invited?*

Suddenly my mood can be shown with a frowning emoticon.

But what can I do? Social media is woven into our culture. Totally unplugging may make my life seem like it's unraveling.

Although we probably won't give up social media, we can do a few things to prevent Facebook envy.

First of all, remember that everyone's life looks better on Facebook. What I post, what you post, are the highlights of our lives. You tell about a great concert you went to or post a smiling picture of yourself with a friend. You don't tell about washing the dishes or upload a picture of yourself with bedhead. Looking at a life in bite-size status updates makes it seem more exciting than it really is. On Facebook, we tend to record the amazing moments of our lives and leave the boring parts out.

Don't let envy build. If you find yourself comparing yourself with all your Facebook friends and losing your joy, log off! Go do something you love. Dance. Run. Read a book. Play the piano—anything that doesn't require a computer or smartphone.

Spend more time with your real friends than your smartphone. Don't let technology control your relationships. Have actual, in-person face time with friends who support you and aren't afraid to be real. Truly connecting with people doesn't happen online.

Most of all, go to God with your envy. You aren't the first person who has struggled with this emotion. Psalm 73 was written by a guy named Asaph who admitted almost losing his faith when he was jealous of people who seemed to have more than he did.

Asaph wrote about two things that freed him from the grip of envy. He realized that although the people he envied seemed to have no problems at all, their lives could change for the worse in an instant (v. 19). Often the things that make envy grip our hearts, the things we wish for, are things that aren't lasting. We can drool over Hollister jeans or the latest iPhone, but in a year or two, they will be yesterday's news. Popularity and success come and go. Is it worth losing your joy over something that won't be around tomorrow?

Asaph also noticed that what really changed his heart was the realization that God was right there with him. At first he was bitter about the good life others had. It made no sense to him (v. 22). But then he understood that the only thing that mattered was that God was there, holding his hand (v. 23). He said, "God is the strength of my heart and my portion forever" (v. 26). God's presence and support were things that could never change or disappear.

When Facebook envy starts to steal your joy, remember where you can find it again. Do something you love that doesn't involve a computer. Hang out with friends in real time. Remember, the things we drool over now probably won't even be around next year. Most of all, connect with God, who promises to be with you forever.

Jesus, thank You that even when I get upset about what I
don't have, You still hold my hand. Remind me that things
I often wish for aren't really lasting, but You will always
be with me. Amen.

"Unlike" Facebook Envy: Four Practical Tips

1. **Limit your computer time.** Set a timer for twenty minutes (or whatever time period you choose). Use that time to cruise Facebook, then get off.

2. **Stop interacting with people who trigger envy.** You know them. The girl who posts pictures of every new outfit. The one who brags about every accomplishment. Hit the hide button.

3. **Go on a technology fast.** Choose one day a week to totally unplug. Use that day to connect with God, nature, family, and friends—without the Internet.

4. **Be careful about what you post.** Are you writing about what a fabulous time you had with one friend, even though it might hurt another friend's feelings? Choose carefully. Ask yourself, "How would I feel if one of my friends posted this?"

Day Two
<><><><><><><><><><><><><><><><><><>
Wardrobe Workout

1. Have you ever had a case of Facebook envy? Talk about the things you see on social media that can make you lol.

2. Read the "'Unlike' Facebook Envy" tips in the sidebar on page 124.

   a. Which tips do you think are useful?

   b. Do you have any other suggestions for avoiding Facebook envy?

3. Read Psalm 73.

   a. Asaph admits to being envious. What kinds of things make him jealous (vv. 3–5, 12)?

   b. What kinds of things make you jealous?

   c. Asaph struggled to understand why it seemed some people had life so much better than others. What finally changed his perspective (v. 17)?

   d. How can being in God's presence change the way we look at life?

4. Get a close-up. Zoom in on one thing you discovered today.

5. Write out our memory verse for this week: "I know how to be brought low, and I know how to abound. In any and every circumstance, I have learned the secret of facing plenty and hunger, abundance and need" Philippians 4:12. Read a phrase, then cover it and write it. Try to write as much of the verse as you can without looking. (You might even want to post the verse on Facebook!)

Day Three

⬦⬦⬦⬦⬦⬦⬦⬦⬦⬦⬦⬦⬦⬦⬦⬦⬦⬦⬦⬦⬦⬦⬦

A Tale of Two Sisters

You covet and cannot obtain, so you fight and quarrel.
You do not have, because you do not ask. James 4:2

A long time ago in a land far away, there were two sisters living in the home of their father. The younger sister was known for her beauty. The older one—not so much. One day, a young man came to visit and fell in love at first sight with one of the sisters. (Guess which one?) Their father gave the young man a job in the family business and eventually got around to asking how he would like to be paid. The young man asked that his pay be the hand of the younger daughter in marriage. (Did you guess right?) The father agreed.

Everything went fine until the wedding day. When it came time for the honeymoon, the father secretly substituted the older sister for the younger one. The young man must have had too much of the wedding punch at the reception, because he didn't notice the switch until the next morning. He angrily confronted the girls' father, who tried to patch up the situation by offering his younger daughter as wife number two!

As you might guess, this story did not end with "and they lived happily ever after."

Perhaps you recognize this tale as the Old Testament story of Jacob. Because of a little sibling rivalry of his own, Jacob ran away from his brother, Esau, and ended up at his Uncle Laban's house. Jacob immediately fell in love with Laban's daughter Rachel (back in those days, it was okay to marry a cousin). He and Laban struck a deal: Jacob would work seven years taking care of Laban's sheep, and then he would marry Rachel. Except Laban tricked Jacob by putting Leah in the wedding dress, and somehow Jacob didn't notice until the morning. When Jacob complained, Laban explained that it was not their custom to let the younger daughter marry before the older. But Laban would let him marry Rachel too—if Jacob would work another seven years. (Having multiple wives was also considered okay back then, but it wasn't God's idea.)

I'm sure you can imagine life in this happy household, with two sisters competing for the love of one man, and one sister clearly the favorite.

Things only got worse when Leah began having children while Rachel's cradle stayed empty. Each woman was envious of what the other had. Leah wanted her husband's love more than anything else, and Rachel was desperate for children. Both women wore their ugliest envy-green outfits and were dreadfully unhappy.

I know they felt awful because I've worn the envy-green outfit too. And whenever I have decided to wear that color, I've been miserable.

Have you noticed this too? Maybe the day starts out great. Your favorite outfit is fresh out of the laundry. Your skin happens to look great today. Even your hair behaves. Plus, today is the day the community theater director is posting the results of the audition for the summer production. You're sure that you will get the lead. You start the day feeling great about yourself. But when you head to the theater, you see a group of friends all gathered around Alyssa, congratulating *her* on getting the starring role. No one even notices you when you press through the crowd to get a look at the list. Of course they wouldn't—you were given only a small part. Suddenly you feel a twinge of envy, and your good mood evaporates.

Now, if we deal with resentment right away, it can lose its grip on our hearts. But too often we are like Leah and Rachel and continue to complain to God that someone else has what we want. We clench our jaws whenever we see the person who has what we desire. We squeeze our hearts shut. Our relationships with God and others begin to fall apart.

But God has an answer for us. In the Book of James, He says:

> What causes quarrels and what causes fights among you? Is it not this, that your passions are at war within you? You desire and do not have, so you murder. You covet and cannot obtain, so you fight and quarrel. You do not have, because you do not ask. James 4:1–2

God tells us, "When you don't get what you want, don't let that eat up your love of life. When someone else gets that thing you want the most, don't allow hatred to build up in your heart. Instead, bring your desires to Me. Ask Me for what you want."

Of course, God is not like a genie who grants our every wish. But opening up our hearts to God changes us. As we honestly bring Him all of our desires, He can help us sort out what will actually bring us joy and what will only make us more miserable. As we concentrate on His goodness, we remember that He wants to give us fabulous blessings—in His timing. We grow in faith.

Maybe the story of Leah and Rachel would have had a happier ending if they had both been able to trust God to give them His richest blessings instead of holding onto envy. But it's not too late for us. When envy starts to fill our hearts, let's remember to open them up to God. Let Him see our deepest desires. Trust Him to give us what is best.

> *Father, You know I sometimes struggle when I see someone else get what I want. Help me to trust that You know my heart's desires even better than I do. Give me the faith and patience to wait for Your timing. In Jesus' name. Amen.*

Loosen Envy's Grip

Envy can lock down our hearts. But we can unlock its grip. Here are a few things you can do when negative feelings begin to build toward a person who has what you want:

- **Realize that things aren't always what they seem.** The person you envy probably has problems of her own.

- **Compliment the person you envy.** This simple act can release envy's hold on you.

- **Pray for the other person.** It's hard to hate someone when you're praying for her.

Remember that you are not necessarily doing these things for the other person. You are doing them to release envy's grip and bring back your own joy.

Day Three
Wardrobe Workout

1. Take this little envy quiz.

   a. If a friend gets the latest iPod, notebook, or phone before you do, it drives you crazy!

   ___ always

   ___ sometimes

   ___ never

b. When you are with friends, you can't help but compare your outfit with what others are wearing.

__ always

__ sometimes

__ never

c. When your friends get good news, you find it hard to be happy for them, because you wish it were happening to you.

__ always

__ sometimes

__ never

d. You get jealous when you find out one of your friends spent time with other people.

__ always

__ sometimes

__ never

e. Finding out about someone else's date can ruin your whole week.

__ always

__ sometimes

__ never

Tally your answers. If most of your answers were "always," you may have a problem with envy. If most of your answers were "sometimes," you are probably working on dealing with envy in a healthy way. If most of your answers were "never," you have conquered envy!

2. Read part of the story of Leah and Rachel in Genesis 29:15–30:8.

   a. Describe the feelings of each sister:

   _____

   _____

   Leah (especially in 29:31–35):

   _____

   _____

   Rachel (especially in 30:1–2):

   _____

   _____

   b. How did envy affect their relationship with each other (30:8)?

   _____

   _____

   with Jacob (30:1–3)?

   _____

   _____

   c. When have you seen envy destroy relationships?

3. Get a close-up. Zoom in on one thing you discovered today.

4. Write out this week's memory verse. Try to do it without looking back at the words.

Day Four

◇◇◇◇◇◇◇◇◇◇◇◇◇◇◇◇◇◇◇◇◇◇◇◇◇◇◇◇◇◇◇◇◇◇

The Color of Contentment

The Lord is my shepherd; I shall not want. Psalm 23:1

When I was a little kid, sitting in church and listening to the pastor read the Bible, I loved it when Psalm 23 was one of the day's lessons. I would look up at the big stained glass window of Jesus holding a little lamb. I could easily picture Jesus as a shepherd playing with the sheep, leading them to a bubbling creek, finding their favorite snack—green grass.

But one part of the psalm always puzzled me: "The Lord is my shepherd; I shall not want." What could that mean? Didn't David want God to be his shepherd? Did he want a different shepherd?

One Sunday after church when Psalm 23 had been part of the service, I asked my mother, "What does that part of that psalm mean—'I shall not want'?"

"Well, it means that because God was David's shepherd, David didn't want anything else."

Hmmm . . . this seemed even more confusing. I was still at the age when I thought my mother knew everything, so I didn't question her. But I didn't understand. Sure, her answer made more sense than not wanting Jesus for a shepherd. But how could David not want anything else? Didn't he want food or clothes? How could you not want chocolaty Fudgesicles or Barbie dolls?

Now that I'm more grown-up, I still love Fudgesicles, but I understand a bit more. David's statement "I shall not want" meant that he was content with what he had. He was saying, "Because God is taking care of me, I have everything I need." He trusted that God would not only provide food and clothes, but rest and comfort, protection and mercy. David was wearing the color of contentment.

When I'm wearing envy green, I'm constantly looking at what I don't have. I'm comparing what I have with what I see others possess. I complain that what I have is not enough.

But on those occasions when I put on the color of contentment, I remember that God has always taken care of me. I begin to trust that Jesus, my Good Shepherd, is leading me on the path that is best for me. Instead of complaining about what I don't have, I start to notice the blessings already within reach.

Contentment doesn't come naturally to me. If I really were a woolly lamb in Jesus' flock, I'd probably be the one saying, "Hey, Shepherd, I know You did Your best in finding us this spot to graze. And yeah, it's got grass to eat and a nice creek to drink from. But there's nothing to do but eat and sleep. I think You could have found a place with a better view. And why does that other sheep get the spot closest to the stream?"

No matter what I have, I always seem to want more. Even though I have a closet full of clothes, I go shopping for *more* clothes. Even though I have great friends, I wish I had *more* friends. *More* seems to be a theme of my life.

Lately, though, I've heard God whispering, *"Enough."* Scripture is clear enough. God is asking me to look at what I already have and realize that it is exactly what I need right now. The Shepherd gently tells me, "I love you. If you needed more, I would give you more. Trust Me—you have enough."

When I struggle to get rid of my envy-green outfit, I try to take myself back to the view of the stained glass window of Jesus holding the little lamb. When I start to look at what I don't have, I remember David's confidence that his Shepherd would give him everything he needed. I repeat his words "The LORD is my shepherd; I shall not want" and ask God to help me wear the color of contentment.

Jesus, my Shepherd, thank You for always providing what I need. Help me to see that what I have right now is enough and that when I need more, You will gladly give it to me. Amen.

When You Struggle with "Enough"

This contentment thing isn't easy. It's hard to say "Enough" when everyone else is saying you need more. If you find yourself struggling with this, here are a few practical steps you might take.

1. **Try a shopping fast.** For one week (or one month) avoid the mall. Shop only for the things you absolutely need (toothpaste, shampoo, etc.). When you don't see the latest styles, you won't even miss them.

2. **Change the subject.** When your friends start discussing their latest shopping trips, turn the conversation to favorite music, books, and movies.

3. **Watch what you watch.** Are there certain magazines, television shows, or Internet sites that make you think, *I wish I had that*? Change the channel. Leave the magazine on the shelf. Click on a site that fuels your contentment instead of your envy.

Day Four
◇◇◇◇◇◇◇◇◇◇◇◇◇◇◇◇◇◇
Wardrobe Workout

1. Let's explore the meaning of contentment.

   a. Look up the word *content* in a dictionary and write the definition below.

   b. Reread the paragraph on page 133 that begins, "But on those occasions . . ." What does that paragraph tell *you* about contentment?

   c. Using what you have learned today, write what *you* think contentment means.

2. Our memory verse this week is Philippians 4:12. Let's look at the verses around it to get more understanding of this verse. Read Philippians 4:10–13. What was Paul's secret for contentment (v. 13)?

3. Get a close-up. Zoom in on one thing you discovered today.

4. Write out the memory verse for this week. No peeking!

Study Styles

A great way to study the Bible is to use symbols to mark key points in the passage.

Read Psalm 23 below and mark it with the following symbols:

Symbol	Where to put it
⑦	by a passage that tells something about God
⑨	by a passage that tells something about me or human nature in general
	by a new discovery
!	by the passage you found most exciting
?	by something you don't understand or want to learn more about

Psalm 23

The LORD is my shepherd; I shall not want.

^{2} He makes me lie down in green pastures. He leads me beside still waters.

^{3} He restores my soul. He leads me in paths of righteousness for His name's sake. ^{4} Even though I walk through the valley of the shadow of death, I will fear no evil, for You are with me; Your rod and Your staff, they comfort me. ^{5} You prepare a table before me in the presence of my enemies; You anoint my head with oil; my cup overflows.

^{6} Surely goodness and mercy shall follow me all the days of my life, and I shall dwell in the house of the LORD forever.

Now use your markings to dive deeper into God's Word. Answer the following questions.

Symbol	Question	Answer
⑦	What does this passage tell you about God?	_____ _____
⑨	What does this passage say about me or human nature in general?	_____ _____ _____
💡	What new discovery did I make?	_____ _____
!	What about this passage is interesting or exciting?	_____ _____
?	What questions do I have? How can I learn more?	_____ _____

Day Five

◇◇◇◇◇◇◇◇◇◇◇◇◇◇◇◇◇◇◇◇◇◇◇◇◇◇◇◇

A Letter to My Young Self

The one who offers thanksgiving as his sacrifice glorifies Me; to one who orders his way rightly I will show the salvation of God! Psalm 50:23

Dear young self,

I know. It's been another disappointing day. You are beginning to wonder if life will ever get better. Everyone around you seems to be more popular, more beautiful, more . . . together.

Sometimes you can't help but feel a stab of envy when guys practically line up to ask out the other girls but barely notice that you exist. You wonder why God didn't make you more athletic or prettier or at least funnier. Maybe then you would get noticed.

But don't get stuck in that "if only" place. God has incredible plans for your life. Just wait.

And while you're waiting, I want you to know three things.

First, I'm going to let you in on a secret: Real life isn't very much like school. Popularity isn't always measured by how hard you can spike a volleyball. The number of friends you have isn't always determined by your clothing size.

Sure. There are models who are successful because of their long legs and eyelashes. A few great athletes will make boatloads of money because of their fast feet and strong arms.

But the world also needs biologists and social workers, math teachers and artists. We need people who can put out fires in buildings and inspire passion in our hearts. We need someone to counsel us when we're confused and heal us when we're sick. God has a place for you in this world. You can be sure of that.

Second, don't envy those who seem to have it all together. The world will not always revolve around them. Even now, they may have problems that you can't see. Perhaps they are in the process of watching their parents' marriage disintegrate or a grandparent die. Maybe they are able to paste on a smiling face every day, but inside they're crying because of their own insecurities.

So don't dwell on what others have. Envy will only eat you up. Wishing you were someone else will devour your heart, bite by bite. Be assured that God made you to be you, and not to be someone else.

Third, be thankful. The best way to a life well lived is to look at everything through a lens of gratitude.

When you're tempted to wish you lived in a big house on the hill like your friend, choose to stop. Find something about your house you like and thank God for it. (Even if the only thing you can come up with right now is your red velvet comforter.)

When you're wishing that the popular girls would invite you to sit with them at the coffee shop, thank God for the friends who always save you a seat in the cafeteria. (Especially for Brianna, who always makes you laugh.)

When you're dreading the gym and once again wondering why God couldn't have made you more coordinated, thank your Creator for the ability to draw or write or play piano. (Maybe you should add a little prayer of thanks that your mother made you take piano lessons. Trust me. All those hours of practice eventually pay off.)

Be thankful, but not because everything is picture-perfect. Be grateful because, even when it's hard to say "Thank You, God," there is something of a miracle in those three words. Gratitude opens our hearts to joy. Thankfulness brings us closer to God. And when you find just one blessing to thank God for, suddenly you will notice another and another. Suddenly life seems not so bad.

Okay, I might as well warn you right now that there will still be bad days. Life won't always be easy. Sometimes you will stumble, but God will be right there to pick you up. When you start to fall, He will grab your hand.

Everything you are going through now actually does serve a purpose. The struggles become the most valuable lessons. The tough times turn out to be when God seems most near.

So thank Him. Thank Him when the day goes well—when you make the team and when you get invited to the party. (Yes, it will happen!) But thank God, too, on the bad days. Thank Him that you are His baptized daughter. Thank Him that He loves you, even if it seems no one else does. Thank Him that He is near. Thank Him that He has a wonderful plan for your life.

Because if you could see your life from where I am now, you would see that God's gifts in Christ keep on coming.

> *Good and gracious God, thank You. Thank You for Your love on the good days and the bad days and everything in between. Give me the lens of gratitude to see the beautiful things in my life, even when it's hard for me to notice them. In Jesus' name. Amen.*

Envy is the art of counting the other fellow's blessings instead of your own.
Harold Coffin[14]

Be Thankful

When you're having one of those days when it's hard to find something to be thankful for, look for some of these blessings in your life:

• a gift God promised in His Word

• a gift of God's presence

• a gift of words

• a gift of taste

• a gift of sound

• a gift of touch

• a gift of laughter

• a gift of color

• a gift very small

• a gift of friendship

• a gift of family

• a gift of hope

• a gift of faith

Day Five
◇◇◇◇◇◇◇◇◇◇◇◇◇◇◇◇◇◇◇◇◇◇◇◇◇
Wardrobe Workout

1. What is your reaction to the quote "Envy is the art of counting the other fellow's blessings instead of your own"?

2. Read Psalm 50:23.

   a. According to this verse, what kind of sacrifice glorifies God?

   b. As Christians, we make sacrifices. What might a sacrifice of thanks-giving look like in your life?

   c. What in your life seems hard right now?

   d. Can you make a sacrifice of thanksgiving? If so, say a prayer right now thanking God for something about this hard thing—the lesson you are learning, the way you see your faith growing, or simply that you know God is with you in the middle of it all.

3. Get a close-up. Zoom in on one thing you discovered today.

4. Write out Philippians 4:12 from memory.

Meaningful Makeover

Envy can make us depressed, angry, and overwhelmed. But regularly practicing thankfulness can help us feel more optimistic, more loving, and less stressed.[15] Experience this for yourself by keeping a gratitude journal this week. Every day, write down three things that you are thankful for.
At the end of the week, answer the questions below.

1. _____
2. _____
3. _____
4. _____
5. _____
6. _____
7. _____
8. _____
9. _____
10. _____
11. _____
12. _____
13. _____
14. _____
15. _____

Questions:

Put an X on the line below that marks your level of contentment now, after keeping this gratitude journal.

●————————————————|————————————————————————●

I'm constantly comparing what   I'm satisfied with
I have with what others have.   what I have.

Compare this with the X you made on Day One. Do you think looking for something to be grateful for every day helped you become more content? Why or why not?

Don't forget to bring your green outfit to your group's meeting!

Fashion
Finesse

A few words about finding the right clothes,
building a wardrobe, and looking your best.

Color Yourself Confident

When you look your best, you feel more confident. So you pick out your favorite fashions, get an awesome hairstyle, and maybe even put on a little makeup. But one thing you may not have considered is the colors you are wearing. An important part of creating your best look is discovering the right colors for you.

To get the real scoop on color, I asked Shari Braendel, author of *Good Girls Don't Have to Dress Bad*, to teach us about choosing the colors that will help each girl shine.

Shari, why is it important to wear the right colors?

Every girl has certain qualities that stand out. The colors she wears should complement these dominant qualities, instead of clash with them. When you walk into a room, you don't want the first thing people notice to be the colors you are wearing. You want them to notice your face.

For instance, a girl with dark hair and light skin looks great in black and white because they coordinate with her dominant color characteristics. But if a girl with blond hair and medium skin tone wears the same black-and-white outfit, it clashes with her coloring. People notice the outfit, but her own beauty fades.

The colors you wear should not speak louder than who you are. You want the colors of your clothing to be a reflection of your beauty.

Can you explain your color system?

The color system is based on each girl's dominant color characteristics. There are six categories.

Clear Girls in this category have a high level of contrast: dark hair, light skin, bright eyes.

Soft Soft coloring has low contrast. The hair and skin have similar intensity: dishwater blond or light brown hair, medium skin tone, medium-colored eyes.

Warm The primary characteristic of this coloring is red or golden-blond hair. A girl with warm coloring may have any color eyes.

Cool This is one color category you girls don't have to worry about yet! Gray or silver-haired women fit in this group.

Deep Girls with deep coloring have dark hair and eyes with light or dark skin tone.

Light The outstanding characteristic of light coloring is very blond hair. "Light" girls may have fair to medium skin and any eye color.

Once we have figured out our best colors, how can we use that information when buying new clothes?

Every season, pick out one neutral and two or three other colors from your color palette. Build your wardrobe around these colors, and you will end up with lots of possibilities for mixing and matching.

What is your best color advice for young women?

Be wary of colors that are trending but don't look good on you. Even if there seems to be a color everyone is wearing, don't wear it if it clashes with your beauty.

If you want to discover your best colors, go to Shari's Color E-nalysis website, www.colorenalysis.com, for a free online color analysis! Use this code, XXX, if you decide to buy color swatches to help you in shopping for your best colors.

Have fun with color. It's a great way to add sparkle and creativity to your wardrobe!

WEEK SIX

Boot Out the Boots of Selfishness and Step Out in Shoes of Love

Memory Verse

By this we know love, that [Jesus Christ] laid down His life for us, and we ought to lay down our lives for the brothers.
1 John 3:16

Day One
These Boots Are Made for Walkin'

By this we know, that [Jesus Christ] laid down His life for
us, and we ought to lay down our lives for the brothers.
1 John 3:16

In the hazy spotlight of the corner streetlamp, three preteen girls moved to the music. Hair flying, arms waving, their feet danced on the concrete driveway to the beat of "These Boots Are Made for Walkin'."

Summer was our season. Mary, Jeanie, and I didn't see much of each other during the school year because we all went to different schools, but come June, we splashed in the neighborhood creek, set up a lemonade stand, and played games in the basement rec room.

One year we had the great idea to put on a show for our parents. We spent a couple of weeks brainstorming ideas for the show, hunting for jokes in old magazines, and rehearsing our skits and dance numbers. Our skits were very sophisticated. In one scene, I was to pretend I was coming into a restaurant. Jeanie took my order and plunked down a bowl of soup on the card table prop. I began to eat, but suddenly stopped and screamed, "Waiter, there's a fly in my soup!" I then yanked a big plastic bug out of the water in the bowl. At every rehearsal, we snorted with laughter. (Go figure.)

We also wanted to be sure to include the old pie-in-the-face gag, but we didn't know what we could use for the pie without letting our parents know what we were up to. Finally we decided that Jeanie would sneak her father's shaving cream out of the bathroom and squirt some into an aluminum pie plate. Poor Mary was the recipient of the eye-stinging mess!

Finally, the big night arrived. The stage? Our driveway. Seating? Lawn chairs. Refreshments? Popcorn and lemonade.

Our big dance number was the finale. As "These Boots Were Made for Walkin'" played, we bobbed our heads. We swung our arms. We moved our feet to the beat as best as we could.

We had a blast, and our parents enjoyed the show. It was an awesome way to spend our summer vacation.

Lately I've been thinking about that old song. It seems to sum up how we sometimes treat the people in this world. Kids push and shove to get to the front of the line. Boots step on toes on the way up the ladder of success. Shoppers get crushed to death at Walmart, just trying to get a few Christmas bargains.

Wearing boots of selfishness and trampling on others to get our own way seems so natural. It's part of our human condition. We all want what we want, and we are often willing to hurt others to get it.

Sometimes I'm surprised at my own selfishness. I hesitate to sponsor a child in Africa who doesn't have enough rice to fill her stomach, even though my fridge is stuffed. I say no to the person asking for volunteers to work at the homeless shelter because I'm too busy cleaning my four-bed-room home.

Even in little things, my selfishness shows up like a persistent visitor. I take the biggest piece of cake. I choose the best seat. I refuse to let the merging car onto the highway in front of me.

Then I read God's Word and I'm humbled. 1 John 3:16 says:

> By this we know love, that [Jesus Christ] laid down His life
> for us, and we ought to lay down our lives for the brothers.

Jesus laid down His life for me, and yet I try to hang onto every dollar. Jesus saw our need and came to save us, and yet I change the channel when the commercials for world relief show starving kids in Africa. Jesus loved me enough to die for me, and yet I'm more likely to kill an hour at the mall rather than use it to serve strangers.

But I want to change. I'm asking God to help me to step out of my boots of selfishness. I want to be the person who notices someone in need and offers to help. I want to be someone who is willing to share the blessings God has given me. I want to be the one who doesn't just talk about the world's problems, but who does something to make a difference.

We're all born with boots made for walkin' over people. We all have a natural tendency to work hard to get what we want, yet ignore the needs of others. But because we have received Jesus' love, the Holy Spirit works in our hearts to change us into people who don't walk *over* others, but walk *to* them in service.

> *Holy Spirit, I can see my selfish heart—a heart that closes its eyes to people who need something from me. Change me. Make me into someone who notices a need and does something about it. In Jesus' name. Amen.*

How many pairs of shoes does the average American woman own?

a. 19

b. 23

c. 57

(Answer: a. 19¹⁶)

Day One

◇◇◇◇◇◇◇◇◇◇◇◇◇◇◇◇◇◇◇◇◇◇◇

Wardrobe Workout

1. Do you own a pair of boots? Bring your boots to your group meeting. Discuss a characteristic of your boots and how this feature could illustrate an aspect of selfishness. (For instance, the fleece lining of a pair of Uggs keeps me warm and comfortable. Selfishness always puts my comfort as the number one priority.)

2. How do you define *selfishness*?

3. What do these verses say about selfishness?

  a. Psalm 119:36 _____

  b. Philippians 2:3 _____

4. What do these verses tell us about giving?

  a. Acts 20:35 _____

  b. 2 Corinthians 9:7 _____

5. Get a close-up. Zoom in on one thing you discovered today.

6. Our memory verse for this week is 1 John 3:16: "By this we know love, that [Jesus Christ] laid down His life for us, and we ought to lay down our lives for the brothers." To help you memorize this passage, call your cell phone from another phone and record the verse in your voicemail or send it to yourself as a text. Also, write the verse below.

Day Two
◇◇◇◇◇◇◇◇◇◇◇◇◇◇◇◇◇◇◇◇◇◇◇
Boots That Pinch

And Jesus, looking at him, loved him, and said to him, "You lack one thing: go, sell all that you have and give to the poor, and you will have treasure in heaven; and come, follow Me." Mark 10:21

I once bought a beautiful pair of brown leather boots. Because I lived in Wisconsin, I needed boots to get me through the snowy winter. But I also wanted to look stylish while walking on my college campus. I thought those boots would be perfect.

But I hardly ever wore them. They turned out to be too tight in the toes and too loose in the heels. And even though the salesman had told me that the leather would stretch to fit my feet perfectly, this never happened. Every time I wore the boots, I ended up with aching toes and blisters on my heels.

Selfishness is like that. The salesmen of the world try to convince me that what I need is to take care of *myself*. Commercials urge me to be self-sufficient and self-indulgent. I can take classes to boost my self-esteem and self-confidence. Amazon has over 300,000 self-help books with titles like *Self-Compassion, Self-Coaching,* and *The Self-Esteem Workbook.* They all promise me that my life will be better if I will only pay attention to my *self.*

But just like the boots that looked good but pinched my toes, selfishness is never that comfortable. Sure, being self-centered may be fashionable. Those self-help products may fix my problems temporarily. But in the end, I discover that self-absorption doesn't truly make me happy.

One day, Jesus met a young man who had a little trouble with selfishness. The Bible doesn't tell us his name, but because he was a wealthy ruler, we'll name him Richard, a good royal name, and call him "Rich" for now. Rich came up to Jesus and asked, "Good Teacher, what must I do to inherit eternal life?" (Mark 10:17). Jesus told him, "You know the commandments: 'Do not murder, Do not commit adultery, Do not steal, Do not bear false witness, Do not defraud, Honor your father and mother'" (v. 19). Rich assured Jesus that he had followed all of those commandments since he was a boy. So far, so good.

Then Jesus looked at him and said, "Good. Then there's just one more thing you need to do. Go and sell everything you have and give it to the poor. Then come and follow Me" (see v. 21). Wouldn't you love to have been there to see Rich's face? I can just imagine his You-have-got-to-be-kidding expression.

Rich couldn't bring himself to follow this instruction. The Bible tells us "he had great possessions" (v. 22). It was too hard for him to give up all his wealth.

I'm not surprised by Rich's reaction. I probably would have done the same.

The thing that does surprise me is the next line in the story: "Disheart-ened by the saying, he went away sorrowful, for he had great possessions" (v. 22). The reason this sentence is so interesting to me is that it goes against our culture.

The world tries to tell us that looking out for number one will make us happy. As long as we concentrate on getting what we want, we will certainly find fulfillment. Hang on to all of your stuff, and you will also hang on to joy.

We may hear the world's message that the path of self will lead to hap-piness; but the point of Rich's story is that, in the end, self-centeredness fails to bring joy, and we go away sad.

I don't think that God is asking all of us to sell everything we have and give it away. But I do think that Rich's story shows us that living for our-selves does not guarantee happiness.

There are seven words in Rich's story that grab my heart every time I read them. Mark 10:21 says, "And Jesus, looking at him, loved him." Even as Jesus was telling Rich to go and sell everything, He was looking at him with love. Can you imagine that look? I like to think that although Rich went away sad, that look of love stayed with him and later motivated him to give everything away and follow Jesus. After all, it is only Jesus' love that can persuade us to follow Him and live unselfishly.

Jesus won't ask all of us to sell everything we have and give it away. But He is asking us to look into His eyes of love and live generously. He knows that a life lived for the self will not bring happiness. But a life lived for Him and for His children will lead to joy.

Don't let the salesmen of the world convince you that the fashionable boots of selfishness will fit you perfectly. You were made to wear the shoes of love.

> *Jesus, thank You for Your love and care. May that love*
> *motivate me to live generously and not selfishly. When*
> *I try to hang on to everything that You have given me,*
> *help me to remember that it is giving that will bring joy.*
> *Amen.*

Six Tips for Finding Boots That Fit!

1. Buy your boots at the end of the day, when your feet are their largest.

2. Most of us have one foot larger than the other. Buy for the larger foot.

3. When you are trying boots on, make sure there is at least a half-inch space beyond your longest toe inside the boot.

4. Don't assume the boots will stretch!

5. The heel should fit comfortably with little or no slipping up and down.

6. Before wearing the boots outside, walk around inside for a while to make sure they are comfortable. Once you wear them outside, you can't return them.

Day Two
Wardrobe Workout

1. The world often urges you to pay attention only to yourself. Today, look for this message in commercials, books, or media. Where did you find it?

2. Read Mark 10:17–22.

   a. What did the young man call Jesus (v. 17)?

b. What does this tell you about how he viewed Jesus?

c. Even though the young man had great wealth, it seems he felt like he needed one more thing. What was it (v. 17)?

d. That one thing is more important than all of our other things. How does that fact help us when we are tempted to hang onto our possessions rather than give them away?

3. Get a close-up. Zoom in on one thing you discovered today.

4. Write out our memory verse for this week: "By this we know love, that [Jesus Christ] laid down His life for us, and we ought to lay down our lives for the brothers" (1 John 3:16). Read a phrase, then cover it and write it. Try to write as much of the verse as you can without looking.

Day Three

◇◇◇◇◇◇◇◇◇◇◇◇◇◇◇◇◇◇◇◇◇◇◇◇◇◇◇◇◇

Be Selfish—With This

For this is the will of God, your sanctification: that you
abstain from sexual immorality; that each one of you
know how to control his own body in holiness and honor.
1 Thessalonians 4:3–4

When I was kid, my mom sometimes let me play with her jewelry.
I could clip on her rhinestone earrings and admire myself in the mirror. I
could pin on a "ruby" brooch or loop some sparkly "jewels" around my neck.
Once in a while, she even let me keep some of her old jewelry with my
dress-up clothes.

But there was one thing she didn't let me play with—her pearl necklace. Besides her wedding ring, it was the only real jewelry she owned. Mom
shared her costume jewelry, but not the piece of value.

We've been talking about how God wants us to live unselfishly. To give
what He has given us. And to find joy in sharing.

But there is one thing that God does not want us to give away freely—
our bodies.

God's design is for each woman to share her body with only one man.
Although our world has totally messed up this whole area of sex, when we
follow God's plan, we are much more likely to have a beautiful sex life. God
wants us to experience intimacy within a committed relationship.

The Creator made us to enjoy sex, but He also knows the painful consequences of sex outside marriage—physical, mental, emotional, and spiritual consequences. He wants you to have a passionate physical relationship
with your husband without all the awful results of giving yourself away too
soon. That's why He wants you to be selfish, so to speak, with your beauty.

In order for you to save your body for your future husband, you will
have to establish some boundaries. If you don't decide ahead of time how far
is too far, your dating relationships can take you where you never planned to
go. (See page 233 for practical guidelines in setting healthy boundaries.)

If you've gone too far before, it's not too late for a fresh start. God continually offers grace to us when we mess up. Ask Him to forgive you and give you the strength to do better next time. Don't focus on past mistakes. Concentrate on the Holy Spirit, who will give you the ability to live in purity.

1 Thessalonians 4:3–8 tells us:

> For this is the will of God, your sanctification: that you abstain from sexual immorality; that each one of you know how to control his own body in holiness and honor, not in the passion of lust like the Gentiles who do not know God; that no one transgress and wrong his brother in this matter, because the Lord is an avenger in all these things, as we told you beforehand and solemnly warned you. For God has not called us for impurity, but in holiness. Therefore whoever disregards this, disregards not man but God, who gives His Holy Spirit to you.

God wants us to be sanctified. Being sanctified means being set apart for a specific purpose. As baptized daughters of God, we have been made special and unique by Him, and He wants us to act that way. He wants the world to see that we are different. What could be more different than staying pure in a sex-crazed world?

1 Thessalonians gives us some specific instructions on living that pure life:

Do: stay away from sexual immorality,
        control your body, and
        live in holiness and honor.
Don't: live in lust like those who don't know Jesus,
        be impure, or
        reject God by ignoring this teaching.

Remember my mother's pearls? When I became an adult, my mother gave me her precious string of pearls. It wasn't that I couldn't have them when I was young. It was that I had to wait until the time was right. If I had played with them when I was little, I might have broken the string or the clasp. Some of the valuable pearls might have been lost.

It's not that God doesn't want you to have sex. He wants you to enjoy beautiful passion when the time is right. But if you play around with sex before that right time, things may get broken. Your heart may be shattered. Your valuable purity may be lost.

So be selfish with the gift of sexuality that God has given you. Save it for the one person who will love you enough to treat you with respect and commit to you for a lifetime. Then you will have the beauty of a passionate physical relationship without the emotional guilt or possible physical problems that come from giving your purity away.

Trust that God knows what He is doing when He says, "Wait." Ask the Holy Spirit to give you the strength to say no. Be selfish with your beauty.

Heavenly Father, thank You for the beautiful gift of sex. Help me to selfishly guard this gift until the time is right to give it away in marriage. Give me the strength to live purely as Your sanctified daughter. In Jesus' name. Amen.

Flee from sexual immorality. Every other sin a person commits is outside the body, but the sexually immoral person sins against his own body. Or do you not know that your body is a temple of the Holy Spirit within you, whom you have from God? You are not your own, for you were bought with a price. So glorify God in your body. 1 Corinthians 6:18–20

Day Three
◇◇◇◇◇◇◇◇◇◇◇◇◇◇◇◇◇◇◇◇◇◇
Wardrobe Workout

1. What is the world's view of sex? What messages do you get about sex from media?

2. Read 1 Thessalonians 4:1–8. Then choose the answer that best completes each statement.

   a. According to verse 1, this whole passage is teaching us how to

      i. obey our parents.

      ii. please God.

      iii. memorize Scripture.

      iv. make pomegranate popsicles.

   b. In verse 3, we learn that one way to please God is to

      i. go to church every Sunday.

      ii. learn how to shear sheep.

      iii. read the Bible every day.

      iv. stay away from sexual immorality.

   c. Verse 8 tells us that if we ignore this instruction about sexual purity, we are ignoring

      i. man.

      ii. society.

      iii. God.

      iv. *Seventeen* magazine.

3. 1 Thessalonians 4:7 says, "God has not called us for impurity, but in holiness." That word *holiness* means we are set apart for a special purpose. We are meant to act differently than those who don't know Jesus. What is one thing you can do this week to demonstrate holiness in the area of sexuality? How can you show others you are different?

4. Get a close-up. Zoom in on one thing you discovered today.

5. Write out this week's memory verse. Try to do it without looking back at the words.

Day Four
◇◇◇◇◇◇◇◇◇◇◇◇◇◇◇◇◇◇◇◇◇◇
Shoes of Sacrifice

Let us not love in word or talk but in deed and in truth.
1 John 3:18

Maddie was taking part in a service project in which five hundred teenagers came together to work in one community. Everyone worked on different home improvement projects for people who were struggling to make ends meet. They built decks and porches, painted fences and walls.

Maddie and her crew were assigned to assist a family who needed their trailer home painted. After three days of painting, they finished the job and moved to another site. However, on the last day of camp, they returned to give the family a housewarming gift, and they received a shock. Here's what happened, in Maddie's words:

> To our surprise, there had been a fire in the resident's home during the middle of the night. Everything was gone. The

entire house was burned from the inside out, and there was only one drawer that did not burn.

In that drawer was the family Bible.

While we thanked God for keeping the family safe, we were in total shock about why something like this would happen to these people who had very little. After many prayers with our resident, our crew decided to hold a freewill offering the last night of camp. The fire department had told us if we raised $2,000, we would be able to purchase a used trailer from them. We told the camp of five hundred teenagers what had happened, and everyone stepped up. Some campers even donated clothes for the children in the family. After the service, we counted all the money, and to our amazement, it totaled $2,025. The family got a new trailer the following week.

I still keep in touch with the youngest daughter. This experience showed me that even when it's hard to understand why things happen, God is there with you every step of the way.

Those teens demonstrated the amazing kind of love and sacrifice that the apostle John talked about:

By this we know love, that [Jesus Christ] laid down His life for us, and we ought to lay down our lives for the brothers. But if anyone has the world's goods and sees his brother in need, yet closes his heart against him, how does God's love abide in him? Little children, let us not love in word or talk but in deed and in truth. 1 John 3:16–18

In a way, Maddie and her friends laid down their lives. They didn't die for the family that lost their home in the fire, but they laid down a part of their lives by giving their time. All of the kids who participated in that service project gave up a week of their summer break. They could have used the time to swim at a beautiful beach or shop in an exciting city. But instead of playing at the beach, they painted houses. Instead of seeing the bright spots of a city, they worked in the darkest areas. They got dirty, worked hard, and slept in sleeping bags on hard floors.

Then, when tragedy struck, they opened their hearts even more and gave some of their money. Money they had planned on spending on themselves they now offered to a family in need. They gave sacrificially.

The teens demonstrated love through their actions. The message in 1 John 3 is "Let's stop *talking* about loving other people; let's *do* something about it!" Maddie and her crew could have simply told the family, "We love you." They could have ended with the part that said, "We'll pray for you." But they *showed* love. They saw a need and did what they could to help.

I'm inspired by these teens. They were willing to do the hard thing. They did what was inconvenient and expensive. They sacrificed in order to show God's love.

God is slowly stretching me to learn to give sacrificially. And I'm finding that this giving doesn't just help those who don't have enough money or food or clothes. It helps me by giving my life meaning and purpose.

God is a God of infinite resources. He could easily make sure that every homeless person had a safe place to live. It would be a cinch for Him to feed all of the hungry children of the world. God doesn't need our help. But He gives us the privilege of working with Him to make those things happen. He knows that our hearts will be blessed when we open them to those in need.

God is also a God of transformation. Although we naturally want to wear the boots of selfishness, our Father gently changes our hearts until we realize how uncomfortable those boots are. He refashions our souls so that wearing the shoes of sacrifice becomes second nature. We can't resist putting on those shoes because of the love that Christ has poured into our hearts.

Let Jesus open your heart to others. Experience the joy that comes when you give a little more than is comfortable. Ask God to show you how you can work with Him to change your corner of the world.

> *Father in heaven, sometimes I close my eyes to the needs I see around me. Help me to open my heart and give, even when it's not easy or convenient. Thank You for giving me the privilege of working with You. In Jesus' name. Amen.*

Living a Life of Love

God's textbook on love in 1 Corinthians 13 teaches practical ideas on how to love others in action:

Love is patient and kind; love does not envy or boast; it is not arrogant or rude. It does not insist on its own way; it is not irritable or resentful; it does not rejoice at wrongdoing, but rejoices with the truth. Love bears all things, believes all things, hopes all things, endures all things. 1 Corinthians 13:4–7

According to God's Word, love is:

patient—Love doesn't snap at her younger brother if she has to wait for him.

kind—Love says "Hi" to the new girl at school and helps her find her way to class.

not arrogant—Love doesn't brag about what she did over the weekend.

not rude—Love listens to others without interrupting with her own stories.

hopes all things—Love realizes that things won't always go her way, but she knows that God has a beautiful plan for her life.

Day Four
◇◇◇◇◇◇◇◇◇◇◇◇◇◇◇◇◇◇◇◇◇◇◇◇◇
Wardrobe Workout

1. God doesn't *need* our help, but He gives us the privilege of working with Him to feed the hungry and help the poor. Why do you think God chooses to work through us?

2. Read 1 John 3:16–18.

   a. What do you think it means to "lay down our lives for the brothers" (v. 16)? Does it always mean dying for someone else?

   b. How can we show that God's love is inside us (v. 17)?

   c. Verse 18 urges us to "not love in word or talk but in deed and in truth."

   Give an example of loving only in *words*:

   Give an example of loving in *action*:

3. Get a close-up. Zoom in on one thing you discovered today.

4. Write out the memory verse for this week. No peeking!

Study Styles

Asking Questions

Any news reporter knows that the key to writing a good article is to ask these questions: Who? What? Where? When? Why? How?

Those same questions can help you to get more out of your Bible reading. Asking yourself a few simple questions will help you dive into the details and discover things you might not notice otherwise.

Read Romans 12:1–13. Invent a question or two in each category. I have given you some to get you started. Then answer the questions to the best of your ability. If you come up with questions you can't answer, talk with your pastor or youth group leader.

What is the theme of the passage?

Where does true change take place (v. 2)?

Who should we love (v. 10)?

When should we be patient (v. 12)?

Why do we serve one another (v. 5)?

How can we live unselfishly (vv. 4–8)?

What _____

_____?

Where _____

_____?

Who _____

_____?

When _____

_____?

Why _____

_____?

How _____

_____?

Day Five
◇◇◇◇◇◇◇◇◇◇◇◇◇◇◇◇
Shoes of Love

*You shall love the Lord your God with all your heart and
with all your soul and with all your strength and with all
your mind, and your neighbor as yourself. Luke 10:27*

"If the shoe fits, buy it in every color." My sister gave me a pillow em-
broidered with those words because she knows I love shoes. It takes a sheer
act of will for me to walk past a store displaying a "SHOE SALE" sign.

But in my spiritual life, I am much more likely to wear boots—the
boots of selfishness. I try to avoid wearing the shoes of love. The boots seem
so comfortable. Loving people often means stepping out of my comfort
zone. It means giving up some of my time or even doing something icky. The
boots of selfishness protect me from stepping into that.

Jesus told a story about someone who wore the shoes of love (Luke
10:25–37). The story explained what it means to love our neighbors.

One day, a man was traveling along a dangerous road. Before he reached
his destination, robbers jumped out, beat him, took his money, and left him
half dead.

Two men who worked at God's temple also happened to be walking on
the road. You would think that they surely would have stopped to help. But
instead of aiding the injured man, they purposely avoided him by walking on
the other side of the road.

Finally, a Samaritan, a person who was despised by the Jews, came by.
Although no one would have expected it, he was the one who stopped to
help. He was the one who showed love. It wasn't easy. Love involved getting down on the ground. It meant getting dirty as he bandaged the man's
wounds. Love required that the Samaritan walk the rest of the way so the
injured man could ride on his animal. It meant giving up some of his own
money to pay an innkeeper to continue the man's care.

Love takes time. Sometimes it's expensive. Often it's messy.

God is slowly working on me in this area of my life. When I'm tempted to walk on the other side of the road and close my eyes to the needs of others, the Holy Spirit gently urges me to take the time to do *something* to help. Lately, one way that I've started to wear the shoes of love is to work for social justice. Some of my friends and I take the time to make and sell bracelets that symbolize the bondage of the 27 million people caught up in modern-day slavery. We spend our own money on the materials so that what we make from selling these bracelets can fund safe houses that shelter women who are rescued from human trafficking.

What about you? What have you been doing to notice the needs of this world and do something to help? While I have heard some people call to-day's young people selfish and entitled, I have seen the opposite. I see young people everywhere stepping up to serve. They are not walking on the other side of the road, ignoring the needs of hurting people. They are willing to give up their time and get messy.

I put out a plea to my Facebook friends for help with this chapter. I asked them to give me examples of teens who serve others, and I received a flood of answers.

- I learned about a teen who breezes into church, still in her Burger King uniform, apologizing for being late. She sits down at her place in front of the computer and calls up the slides and videos for the evening service. She seldom receives thanks, but she humbly serves.
- Matthew volunteered to be a Best Buddy at his school. Every day, he helped a handicapped student in science class and sat with him at lunch. Matthew loved the experience.
- Anthony organized a group of teens to drive to a town two hours away that had been devastated by a tornado. The teens cut trees and moved debris. It was hard, dirty, and dangerous work.
- Adam and his brother Sam regularly bring music to a local nursing home. Adam plays the piano and Sam sings. They receive only the gratitude of the residents.
- Three brothers take turns shoveling the driveway of an elderly neigh-bor. They don't get any medals or trophies, but they do it anyway.
- Brianna, Beth, and the rest of their youth group go on a service trip every year. They work in a poor community, repairing sagging porches, building wheelchair ramps, and doing general home repairs.

It isn't glamorous work, but it helps the residents who don't have the funds to fix their homes.

All of these young people have walked on the difficult side of the road. They saw a need and *did something.*

So keep serving! Share some of your time and money. Get messy. Wear the shoes of love.

> *Dear Father, so many times when I look down at my feet, I am still wearing the boots of selfishness. I want to wear the shoes of love. Help me be willing to share what You have given me and love others, even when it's messy or hard. In Jesus' name. Amen.*

There are two things you can never have too many of: good friends and good shoes.

Prayer in action is love, and love in action is service. Try to give unconditionally whatever a person needs in the moment. The point is to do something, however small, and show you care through your actions by giving your time.

Mother Teresa[17]

Day Five
◇◇◇◇◇◇◇◇◇◇◇◇◇◇◇◇◇◇◇◇◇◇◇◇◇◇
Wardrobe Workout

1. How have you worn the shoes of love? How have you helped others in need?

2. Read the story of the Good Samaritan in Luke 10:25–37.

    a. Jesus told this story to better explain the commandment "Love your neighbor as yourself." What do you think it means to love your neighbor as *yourself*?

    b. An expert in the law asked Jesus, "Who is my neighbor?" (v. 29). Why do you think he asked that question?

    c. According to the story, who is our neighbor? Is it always someone who lives next to us?

3. Get a close-up. Zoom in on one thing you discovered today.

4. Write out 1 John 3:16 from memory.

Meaningful Makeover

This week we have talked about laying down our lives for others. Laying down our lives doesn't necessarily mean dying for them. It can mean doing something hard, something messy, something that doesn't give us a reward. Meditate on 1 John 3:16 once again:

By this we know love, that [Jesus Christ] laid down His life for us, and we ought to lay down our lives for the brothers.

How can you lay down your life for your family? your friends? your community? the world? Brainstorm some ideas.

Family:_____

_____

Friends:_____

_____

Community:_____

_____

The world:_____

_____

Circle one of your ideas and plan to do it this week!

Remember to bring your boots to your group's meeting!

**A few words about finding the right clothes,
building a wardrobe, and looking your best.**

A Pair of Shoes

Do you know how to pair the right shoes with the right outfit? Although modern fashion rules are almost nonexistent, sometimes it's helpful to have a little guidance in knowing which shoes to wear when.

Here are a few general guidelines:

- Choose shoe colors that match your outfit rather than compete with it, especially if the occasion is serious or professional.

- On the other hand, for fun times, choose a bright color to add pop to a plain outfit.

- Keep in mind where you are wearing the shoes. Choose a style that won't kill your feet if you have to walk a mile! Choose comfort over style.

- Four-inch heels may be stylish, but if you can't walk in them, the look won't be so impressive. Stick to shoes that make you feel comfortable and confident.

And here are a few specific fashion guidelines:

Flats Wear flats with knee-length skirts, ankle-length pants, or jeans. Flats can be basic black, blend-in-brown, or charmingly colorful. Pick the color to suit the occasion or your mood.

Heels Wear high heels with slim skirts and pants. Wear heels for formal occasions.

Sandals Dressy sandals are great for formal events. Save flip-flops for casual settings.

Sneakers Wear athletic shoes when you are wearing workout clothes. (Duh.) Avoid wearing sneakers with dressier clothing. **Wear casual sneakers rather than high-tech running shoes with jeans.**

Boots Wear boots with jeans, and winter coats.

For fun contrast, wear cowboy boots with a floral dress. Boots are attention getting, so wear them when you want to make a fashion statement.

Shoes are an essential part of any wardrobe, but they can also make fashion fun. Find the shoes that show off your style!

WEEK SEVEN

Unravel the Bitterness Sweater and Choose to Wear Forgiveness

Memory Verse

Be kind to one another, tenderhearted, forgiving one another, as God in Christ forgave you. Ephesians 4:32

Day One

<>><><><><><><><><><><><><><><><><><><><><><><><><><>

Wrapping Up in Bitterness

Let all bitterness and wrath and anger and clamor and
slander be put away from you, along with all malice. Be
kind to one another, tenderhearted, forgiving one another,
as God in Christ forgave you. Ephesians 4:31–32

Graduation was near. My last year of high school was winding down. It was the end of an awesome year. Classes were going well. Playing in the band at football games and concerts with my friends had been a blast. I had awesome times with my two best friends, Deb and Barb, sharing laughter and dreams.

As the school year came to a close, I kept my eyes on my goal: maintaining my grade point average so I could be one of the graduation speakers. I was sure that I would be picked for one of the two speaking spots. Looking back, I'm not sure why this was so important to me, but it was. I wanted to be standing at the podium in my cap and gown on the big night.

But it was not to be. Instead, I was told, "Yes, your grade point was good, but this year we decided to take extracurricular activities into consideration as well. So we've chosen Deb."

I was angry. Sure my friend Deb was more talented and more involved in school activities, but I had concentrated on my grades to achieve my goal. Then the rules were changed, and I was left out. It wasn't fair.

To make matters worse, I let my anger at the school officials spill over to my friend. I should have immediately congratulated Deb. Okay, I really couldn't be *excited* for her, but our friendship should have been more important to me than a speech. But somehow I couldn't let it go. I stubbornly avoided Deb, fumed about the graduation ceremony, and silently complained about the unfairness of it all. I even secretly hoped her speech would be a flop. (It turned out to be moving and inspiring.)

I grabbed onto bitterness and wrapped it tightly around my heart.

We've all been hurt. People ignore us. Friends say things that stab us like a knife. Girls we thought we could trust spill our secrets.

And that's when we tend to put on the bitterness sweater. We somehow think that it will comfort us against a chilly world. We store up all our angry feelings, playing them over and over in our minds. We pull bitterness tighter and tighter, unwilling to let mercy get close to our hearts.

But after a while, we discover that bitterness isn't comfortable at all. It's more like an itchy wool sweater that feels good when we first put it on, but gradually becomes more and more irritating. Bitterness scratches our spirits. It scrapes our souls.

God tells us that we should wear forgiveness instead:

> Let all bitterness and wrath and anger and clamor and slander be put away from you, along with all malice. Be kind to one another, tenderhearted, forgiving one another, as God in Christ forgave you. Ephesians 4:31–32

God wants us to take off bitterness and put on forgiveness. We might think that bitterness will make us feel better. It will be like a shield around our damaged hearts. It will comfort our hurt feelings.

But *forgiveness* is what actually frees our aching souls.

After that painful graduation night, my friend Deb and I went our separate ways. I tried to ignore that tight spot in my heart where I still held a grudge. After a time, I didn't notice it much anymore. But a couple of years later, Deb and I ended up at the same college, and I realized that my bitterness was still there. In order to get rid of the pain in my heart, I had to learn to forgive. I had to forgive the school officials who chose Deb over me. I had to let go of my bitterness toward Deb. After all, she had done nothing wrong.

One day I worked up my courage and phoned Deb. I asked if we could meet. Her voice sounded unsure of what to expect, but she said yes. When I got to her apartment, I told her that I was sorry that I had let my fixation on a speech wreck our friendship. I let her know that I had let go of the bitterness I felt about the whole situation. Would she forgive my stupidity?

Deb graciously said yes.

After I took off that bitterness sweater, I realized what a tight hold it had had on my heart. Now that I had forgiven and had been forgiven, I felt the tightness in my soul loosen.

Jesus wants all of us to experience that freedom of forgiveness. He modeled this Himself by taking our sins and mistakes to the cross and erasing them. And because He has forgiven us, we can extend His mercy to others. At His Table, He wraps us in forgiveness that comforts like nothing else can.

Jesus, thank You for taking all of my sins to the cross and forgiving them. Help me to pass on forgiveness to the people around me instead of holding on to bitterness. Thank You for Your mercy and grace. Amen.

Sweater Styles

Do you know your sweater styles? Match up the name of the sweater with the correct description.

1. cable-knit sweater

2. Fair Isle sweater

3. cardigan sweater

4. cowl-neck sweater

5. wrap sweater

6. pullover

a. opens down the front

b. put on over the head

c. has wrap-over fronts secured with a belt or ties

d. knit with a twisting pattern

e. has a geometrical pattern

f. has a neckline that drapes in rounded folds

(Answers: 1. d; 2. e; 3. a; 4. f; 5. c; 6. b)

When your friends let you down, you don't have to be best friends with them anymore. But you can let it go. You don't have to worry about it anymore.

Brianna

Day One

◇◇◇◇◇◇◇◇◇◇◇◇◇◇◇◇◇◇◇◇◇

Wardrobe Workout

1. Which sweater are you most likely to wear: the warm-but-scratchy bitterness sweater or the softer-than-cashmere forgiveness sweater? Look through your wardrobe to find a sweater that symbolizes your usual reaction to people who hurt you. Bring your sweater to your group meeting.

2. Bitterness is stored anger. How do you deal with anger? Write out the following verses and mark on the scale where you see your usual response to anger, with 1 being lowest and 10 being highest.

   Proverbs 16:32:

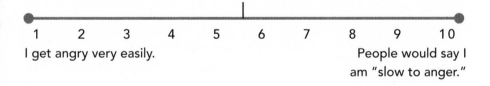

   1   2   3   4   5   6   7   8   9   10
   I get angry very easily.   People would say I
                                                   am "slow to anger."

   1 Corinthians 13:4–5:

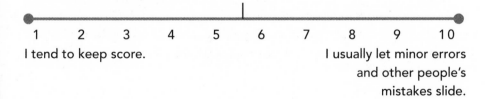

   1   2   3   4   5   6   7   8   9   10
   I tend to keep score.   I usually let minor errors
                                                   and other people's
                                                   mistakes slide.

Romans 12:19:

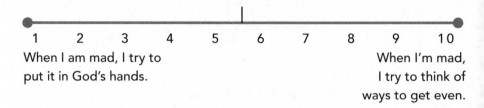

| 1 | 2 | 3 | 4 | 5 | 6 | 7 | 8 | 9 | 10 |

When I am mad, I try to
put it in God's hands.

When I'm mad,
I try to think of
ways to get even.

3. Which of the preceding passages will help you most the next time you
   are angry?

   Turn that verse into a prayer. Write it below.

4. Get a close-up. Zoom in on one thing you discovered today.

5. Our memory verse for this week is Ephesians 4:32: "Be kind to one
   another, tenderhearted, forgiving one another, as God in Christ forgave you." To help you memorize this passage, write the words on a
   sticky note and put it on your sweater drawer. Also, write it out in the
   space below.

Day Two
◇◇◇◇◇◇◇◇◇◇◇◇◇◇◇◇◇◇◇◇◇◇◇
Be Angry. Don't Sin.

Be angry and do not sin; do not let the sun go down on
your anger, and give no opportunity to the devil.
Ephesians 4:26–27

Torry and her parents were having a discussion about her friends—
again. Torry was spending the day with some new kids she had met at
school, but her parents had questions. "It's not that we don't trust you," they
told her, "but we don't know if we can trust the other kids."

The friends you hang with. The food you eat. The clothes you wear.
Where you go. What time you come home.

All of these are potential topics of discussion with your parents.

When you were little, your mom and dad had control over all those
things. They fed you, picked out your clothes, and arranged play dates.

But now you're older. As a part of maturing, you are learning to make
good decisions. Now you choose what you wear and who your friends are.
You don't want your parents telling you what to do.

Every one of those topics could be an anger trigger.

In fact, as a young woman, you may have noticed that you get mad
more often than you used to. You don't even want that emotion, but sometimes it's there whether you like it or not.

So how can you deal with it?

Ephesians 4:26–27 gives us a little lesson in anger management:

> Be angry and do not sin; do not let the sun go down on your
> anger, and give no opportunity to the devil.

Right away I notice something interesting. It says, "Be angry. Don't sin."
Anger itself is not a sin. It's just an emotion. But anger can be such a strong
emotion that it can make us do things we regret later. Things like yelling at
our parents, hurting them with our words, or purposely disobeying them to
get back at them.

Ephesians also tells us to not let the sun go down on our anger. In other words, try to deal with anger right away. Continually holding onto anger can create a bitter heart. Bitterness is essentially stored anger. And while it's good to save up money and stow away our clothes, it's not a good idea to hold onto anger.

Stored anger is a little like the air inside a balloon. Each time we save up a little more bitterness and resentment, we put a little more air inside the balloon. Eventually the balloon will break. Anger will explode everywhere. And it won't be pretty.

The final lesson in anger management from Ephesians is "Give no opportunity to the devil." Now what does *that* mean? I'm sure you don't picture yourself opening the door of your room to Satan and giving him an opportunity to talk you into doing something you will later wish you hadn't. But in a way, that's what anger does. It lets Satan put his foot in the door and it makes it a little easier for him to get you to listen to him. When you're mad, it takes much less effort on Satan's part to get you to lash out at those you actually love.

How can we deal with feelings of rage without stuffing them back down inside of us or exploding in a very messy way?

I find it helpful to look at the emotion. Imagine you could pull the anger out of you and put it in a box—for now. Remind yourself it's just an emotion. It doesn't define you; it's not who you are.

Then mentally place that box of anger in God's hands. Honestly tell Him all about your angry feelings. He can handle it. Let God know you're not sure what to do with the emotion. Ask Him for His help.

Now take a closer look at the emotion. Mentally, let God open the box, and together, examine its contents. Ask yourself, "What am I really angry about? Why did this make me so mad?" Torry was angry that her parents questioned her about her new friends. She felt it meant that they didn't trust her judgment—her choice of friends. She was angry that she might miss out on fun; she also worried that if she didn't spend time with them, she wouldn't be popular.

When you have cooled down, talk about the issue with the other person. But remember that be-angry-and-do-not-sin thing. No name-calling. No hurtful words. Calmly talk about how you feel and why you feel that way. Torry told her parents about her frustration.

Hear the other person's side. Really try to see things from their point of view. Parents naturally want to protect their children. Torry's parents knew that people who seem okay at first sometimes turn out to be trouble.

Torry and her parents worked out a solution to the friend problem. They invited all of Torry's friends over for a bonfire. Once Torry's parents got to know the new friends, they were comfortable with Torry spending long periods of time with them.

Learning to deal with anger is an important part of becoming an adult. Fortunately, the Holy Spirit is right there when we need Him to help us sort out our feelings. He can help us pinpoint the problem and then go to the other person and work things out.

Remember: anger is a feeling. On its own, it's not a sin. But it can make us do some terrible things. Things we will later regret.

Be angry. Don't sin.

> *Holy Spirit, sometimes anger builds up in me and I just don't know what to do with that feeling. Help me to turn to You when I'm mad. Show me how to deal with my anger without hurting others. In Jesus' name. Amen.*

Healthy Ways to Deal with Anger

- **Exercise**—Physical activity can help you burn up some of your pent-up emotion.

- **Write**—Journaling about your feelings can help you understand them better.

- **Draw**—Art can be a way to express your feelings in a non-hurtful manner.

- **Music**—Listen to loud music that expresses your frustration, and then switch to something quiet to calm yourself down.

Day Two

◇◇◇◇◇◇◇◇◇◇◇◇◇◇◇◇◇◇◇◇◇◇◇◇◇◇◇◇

Wardrobe Workout

1. What are some of the topics you and your parents sometimes discuss?

2. How do you deal with anger? What works for you to calm down?

3. King David begins many of his psalms by pouring out his anger to God. Psalm 55 is one of those psalms. Read it and answer the questions below.

   a. What had happened that made David so angry (vv. 12–14, 20–21)?

   b. Have you ever experienced a friend's betrayal?

   c. To get beyond the anger, David reminds himself of how God will help him. What are some things God does for us?

verses 16–17 _____

verse 18 _____

verse 22 _____

verse 23 _____

    d. Which of those things might help you the most when you've been hurt by a friend?

4. Get a close-up. Zoom in on one thing you discovered today.

5. Write out our memory verse for this week: "Be kind to one another, tenderhearted, forgiving one another, as God in Christ forgave you" (Ephesians 4:32). Read a phrase, then cover it and write it. Try to write as much of the verse as you can without looking.

Day Three
◇◇◇◇◇◇◇◇◇◇◇◇◇◇◇◇◇◇◇◇◇◇◇◇◇
Unraveling Bitterness

And we know that for those who love God all things work together for good, for those who are called according to His purpose. Romans 8:28

Try to imagine that you are a teenage boy in a big family. In fact, you have a ton of older siblings—brothers who take great delight in torturing you. They seem to think you get a little too much attention from Dad, and they're trying to make your life miserable.

One day when your brothers are all at work at the family business, your father asks you to go and check up on them: "Go see if they're okay." So you pack a lunch and set out to pay them a surprise visit.

But you're the one who ends up being surprised. They must have seen you coming because before you can even say hello, your older brothers grab you and throw you into a hole in the ground. A hole so deep and dark you can't get out.

You knew your brothers hated you, but—really? Throw you into a *hole?*

And there you sit. You know they're still up there; you can hear them talking, but you can't make out what they are saying. Then you hear some new voices—voices with strange accents. Apparently the family has visitors.

The voices come nearer. "Come on," you hear one of your brothers say. "Let's get him out of there."

Two of your brothers yank you out by your armpits and shove you toward the strangers.

"Here," they tell the strangers. "Now he's *your* problem."

The strangers tie your hands behind your back and drag you away. *What will happen now?*

* * * * * *

You might have recognized this as the story of Joseph. Joseph was probably about your age when his brothers sold him to a group of wandering traders who took him to Egypt, hundreds of miles from home. Joseph may have had to walk the whole way; and when he got there, he was sold as a slave.

At first, life as a slave wasn't so bad. Joseph worked for a high-ranking government official who recognized Joseph's potential and treated him well. But then there was that misunderstanding with the official's wife (Genesis 39), and Joseph ended up in a dark Egyptian prison for more than two years.

I don't know about you, but I would have been more than a little miffed at my brothers if I had been Joseph.

Eventually, though, Joseph was released from prison because God gave him the ability to explain Pharaoh's unusual dreams. Joseph predicted seven years of plenty and seven years of famine. Pharaoh recognized Joseph's wisdom and made him second-in-command. Joseph was put in charge of storing food during the years of good crops and of selling the stored food during the years of famine.

Joseph didn't see his family for seventeen years, not until the seven years of famine arrived. When Joseph's family ran out of food, the brothers heard there was food in Egypt and traveled there to get some. Joseph recognized them, but of course they didn't know him. How could they have suspected that their little brother now would be an important part of a world power?

Joseph now had a choice. Would he let go of all his bitterness and forgive his brothers? Or would he hold onto anger and work a little revenge?

At first, it seemed as if Joseph might be bent on revenge. When the brothers asked for food, he accused them, "You are spies; you have come to see the nakedness of the land" (Genesis 42:9). Joseph treated them like strangers and even put one of the brothers in jail. (There, see how *you* like Egyptian prisons!)

Perhaps Joseph had been storing up more than grain during the seven years of good crops. He had also been holding on to anger. But it's interesting to see that bitterness did not make him happy. Even as he had Simeon bound and taken to prison, Joseph turned away and started to cry (v. 24).

Joseph didn't forgive his brothers until the second time they came to Egypt. After making them suffer a little more by making it look like the youngest brother had stolen a valuable silver cup, he finally came clean. He said:

> I am your brother, Joseph, whom you sold into Egypt. And now do not be distressed or angry with yourselves because you sold me here, for God sent me before you to preserve life. Genesis 45:4–5

Joseph made the choice to forgive. Bitterness was only causing more pain. Holding on to the hurt was making him miserable.

How could he let it go? By realizing that even in the hurt, God had a purpose for his life. The years of slavery and imprisonment were no fun, but in the end, God used all the horrible experiences to save lives. Joseph's plan to store grain enabled many people to have food when there was none in the fields. And his plan allowed him and his brothers to reconcile.

When people wound us, it's hard to find anything good in the pain. But it helps to remember that God is right there with us in the hurt. And He doesn't allow any heartache without a plan; He uses every rotten circumstance and lovingly turns it into something good.

Right now it might be hard to see how anything good can come out of something like a friend's betrayal. But Jesus can work wonders. He can unravel our bitterness. As we receive His forgiveness through His body and blood, we can pass it on to those who have hurt us.

Jesus releases our hearts from bitterness and transforms our pain into purpose.

God of purpose, I know that You don't allow anything in my life without a plan. Unravel my bitterness. Help me to see the good that can come out of painful times. In Jesus' name. Amen.

Refashion a Sweater

We've been talking about unraveling the bitterness sweater. But you can also have fun recycling the old sweaters in your drawer. Here are a few ideas.

- **Headband**—Cut off the bottom six inches of a sweater. Fold in half lengthwise. Adjust the length to fit your head and do a little sewing.

- **Boot socks**—Cut the sleeves off a colorful patterned sweater. Wear under boots like leg warmers.

- **Mittens**—Trace a mitten shape around your hand on a piece of paper. Using the bottom of the sweater as the cuff, cut out four pieces from your pattern. Sew two together for each hand and add a button for fun.

Find instructions and more ideas by doing an Internet search of "recycling sweaters."

That's what keeps me going—knowing that everything will work out in the end.
Beth

Day Three
Wardrobe Workout

1. Put yourself in Joseph's shoes. How would you have handled the meeting with your brothers when they came for food?

2. Read Genesis 45:1–11.

   a. Why do you think Joseph's brother were terrified of him (v. 3)?

   b. How did Joseph calm them down (v. 5)?

   c. What purpose did Joseph see in his brothers' betrayal (vv. 5–7)?

   d. Think back to a tough time in your life—perhaps a time when some-one hurt you. Can you now see something good that came out of that time?

3. Get a close-up. Zoom in on one thing you discovered today.

4. Write out this week's memory verse. Try to do it without looking back at the words.

Day Four
The Choice of Forgiveness

And whenever you stand praying, forgive, if you have anything against anyone, so that your Father also who is in heaven may forgive you your trespasses. Mark 11:25

Forgiveness is a choice.
Read that statement again. Does it surprise you?
When we are hurt, we grab that bitterness sweater. Sometimes we wrap

it around our hearts and refuse to let go of our anger. We can't even think of forgiving the people who hurt us. They don't deserve it. There's no way they should be given mercy. We certainly do not feel like forgiving them.

But forgiveness doesn't start with an emotion. It starts with a choice.

Jesus told His disciples, "Whenever you stand praying, forgive, if you have anything against anyone" (Mark 11:25). He didn't say, "When you *feel* like forgiving the friend who turned on you, forgive her" or "If the rat who broke your heart is truly sorry, let him off the hook" or "After the mafia has broken all his bones to even up the score, go ahead and forgive."

Jesus simply said, "If you have anything against anyone, forgive. If you have been hurt, forgive. If the other person isn't sorry, give him grace anyway. If you are still feeling miserable about what happened, let it go."

Jesus showed how to give this kind of mercy. He was arrested on made-up charges, ridiculed, mocked, and beaten with whips. Although He had done nothing wrong, He was sentenced to death. And even while Roman soldiers were pounding spikes into His hands and feet, He said, "Father, forgive them, for they know not what they do" (Luke 23:34). Jesus made the choice to forgive.

He asks us to make that choice too. He wants us to make that choice because He knows it will free our hearts. Hanging onto anger makes us feel like we are doing something to punish those who hurt us. We silently whip them with our icy silence. We beat them with our stony words. We imprison them with our anger.

But in the end, we are the ones who are caged by our bitterness. Holding onto the hurt only deepens the pain. Grasping onto anger holds our souls captive.

Unforgiveness also blocks our relationship with God. Jesus went on to say that we should forgive "so that your Father also who is in heaven may forgive you your trespasses" (Mark 11:25). If I refuse to give mercy to others, God will also hold back His grace from me. There will be a wall between me and God. Actually, there has already been that wall between us and God, and God has torn it down through Jesus' death on the cross. My soul is free in God's grace so that now I can choose to forgive in the abundance of God!

The choice of forgiveness isn't an easy one to make. But we don't necessarily do it for the other person—we do it because of Jesus. We know that if we don't forgive, we will continue to feel trapped by anger and sin. We also do it because Jesus tells us to and because only forgiveness can free us from sins—our own or those against us.

So how do we go about this forgiveness thing? These steps may help:

1. **Ask God to help you to forgive.** Forgiveness is hard, often impossible, to do on our own.

2. **Write about it.** Try writing what the other person did on a piece of paper. Now look at what you wrote and tell God, "Lord, I forgive her."

3. **Destroy the piece of paper.** Rip it into tiny pieces, put it through the shredder, burn it in the fireplace—anything to symbolize that you are no longer holding on to that hurt.

4. **The next step depends on your situation.** If the other person has asked for forgiveness or said she was sorry, then go to her and let her know you have forgiven her. But if she isn't really sorry for the pain she caused or isn't even aware that she has done something hurtful, you probably won't want to confront her. It might make matters worse. But you could write a letter—a letter you won't send—telling her you have forgiven her for the hurt she brought to your life. This letter would be for your eyes only, but it would help you feel like you have shut the door on that hurt.

Repeat these steps whenever anger starts to boil up again.

Because the choice of forgiveness is not based on our feelings, it's a choice we may have to make over and over again. When our options are bitterness or forgiveness, we choose option number two because we have received forgiveness from Jesus. He asks us to pass it on because He knows that bitterness will cage our souls. Live free in God's grace.

> *Author of forgiveness, thank You for Your example of mercy in spite of pain. Help me to follow Your Word instead of my feelings. Help me to choose to forgive. Amen.*

Forgiving . . . Yourself

Sometimes the person you find it hardest to forgive is yourself. When you've blown it. When you've totally messed up. When you've done something you know your parents, your pastor, your Savior wouldn't approve.

You don't know what to do. You find yourself in an I-feel-so-guilty prison.

You don't have to stay there.

Ask God for His grace. Because of Jesus' death and resurrection, God forgives all of our mess-ups—big and small.

Ask others for forgiveness. If you have hurt someone else, go to them and ask for his or her forgiveness too.

Hang onto God's promise of mercy and grace: "If we confess our sins, He is faithful and just to forgive us our sins and to cleanse us from all unrighteousness" (1 John 1:9. See also Romans 8:1; Psalm 32:1–5.)

To forgive is to set a prisoner free and discover that the prisoner was you.[18]
Lewis B. Smedes

Day Four

Wardrobe Workout

1. Write your reaction to this statement: Forgiveness doesn't start with an emotion. It starts with a choice.

2. Read Mark 11:24–25.

    a. Jesus talks about two important parts of prayer in these verses. What are they?

    b. Why is forgiveness an important part of prayer?

3. Get a close-up. Zoom in on one thing you discovered today.

4. Write out the memory verse for this week. No peeking!

Study Styles

An excellent way to understand a passage is to put it in your own words. Let's do this with these verses about forgiveness: "Put on then, as God's chosen ones, holy and beloved, compassionate hearts, kindness, humility, meekness, and patience, bearing with one another and, if one has a complaint against another, forgiving each other; as the Lord has forgiven you, so you also must forgive" (Colossians 3:12–13).

Using a dictionary and thesaurus (paper or digital), find definitions and synonyms for the following key words from our verse. (Note: Most words will have a long list of definitions or synonyms. Choose the ones that best fit the words in this passage.)

Compassionate _____

_____

Kindness _____

_____

Humility _____

_____

Meekness _____

_____

Patience _____

_____

Bear (verb) _____

_____

Forgive _____

_____

Now, using your definitions and synonyms, write Colossians 3:12–13 in
your own words.

Day Five
◇◇◇◇◇◇◇◇◇◇
Button Up

Whoever covers an offense seeks love, but he who repeats a matter separates close friends. Proverbs 17:9

Imagine this story: Amber and Lily had been best friends since fifth grade. They used to do everything together: homework, shopping, youth group. But since they started high school, they hadn't see each other as much. Amber had found a new passion in theater—she was a part of every school play. Lily was insanely busy with the track team and pom-pom squad.

Still, Amber missed her friend and decided that they needed to reconnect. So she texted Lily and arranged a day to meet at the mall. Amber couldn't wait to cruise the shops and share news about their lives over tacos.

On Saturday, Amber headed to the mall and waited in the food court for her friend. Ten minutes went by, then fifteen. After waiting for twenty minutes, Amber texted Lily, "Where r u?"

A few minutes later, Lily texted back, "Sry! I 4got!"

At first, Amber tried to not let it bother her, but she later found out from a mutual friend that on that particular Saturday, Lily had been with Jessie, a popular girl at school. Now it took real effort to forgive. Lily had not simply forgotten; she had chosen a new friend over Amber.

Eventually Amber decided to let it go. Holding onto anger wasn't going to make things any better. But every time Amber saw Lily with Jessie, it felt like a new stab to her soul.

* * * * * * *

Even after we have made the choice to forgive, things will happen to reignite the hurt. Satan will try to get us to wear anger again. And again.

So we need to button up the sweater of forgiveness a little tighter. If we have it buttoned up tight, it will be harder for us to go back to wearing bitterness. Here are three buttons that will help us keep wearing the sweater that God wants us to wear.

Button up your mind. After you have made the decision to forgive, choose not to dwell on the problem. Instead, choose to focus on something positive about the other person—or focus on what you can learn from the situation.

In our story, it would have been easy for Amber to keep thinking about Lily's choice. She could have even started to obsess about it: *How could Lily forget me? Why did she choose another friend over me? How could Lily be so rude?*

But none of those thoughts would make the situation any better. Instead, Amber could remember the good times with Lily and acknowledge that friendships change over time. If she held onto her anger, she would not be able to form new friendships herself.

Button up your lips. Don't keep talking about the problem! Yes, it might be helpful to talk about the hurt you experience with a parent or a close friend, but don't discuss the problem over and over. Constantly talking about the issue will only amplify it. *Not* obsessing about it will help you forget it.

It would have been tempting for Amber to tell all of her other friends about how Lily had ignored her. The friends might have been supportive at first, but after awhile, they probably would have grown tired of talking about it. They might even have started avoiding Amber. Plus, Amber's bitterness would have continued to grow whenever she brought up the subject.

Button up with prayer. Forgiveness isn't easy. We need God's help. Whenever you're tempted to put on the bitterness sweater, say a prayer asking God to help you forgive once again.

Also pray for the person who hurt you. Jesus said, "But I say to you, Love your enemies and pray for those who persecute you" (Matthew 5:44).

Of course, there is a right way and a wrong way to do this. If I were in a situation like Amber's, my natural reaction would be to pray something like this:

"Lord, make Lily trip on the track at her next meet."

"God, make all of Lily's new friends ignore her."

"God, strike her with leprosy." (That sounds sorta biblical, right?)

But of course, that kind of prayer is not part of forgiveness.

Instead, when you pray, ask that God would take care of the problem between the two of you. Pray for the other person's relationship with God. Pray for God's blessings on the other person.

A funny thing happens when you talk to God about someone. It's very hard to stay angry. The resentment melts away.

People will hurt us. Sometimes the hurt will be intentional. Sometimes they won't even know that they caused us pain. But when we experience heartache, we have a choice. We can make it worse by constantly thinking about it and talking about it over and over again. Or we can let it go. We can take the problem to God and, by His grace, even pray a blessing on the one who caused the pain.

Our Savior knows all about pain. Remember how His disciples betrayed Him before He was arrested and crucified? Jesus is there to listen to us. He can cover over the hurt with His love and help us move forward in life.

Giver of grace, take the bitterness from my heart and cover it with love. Untangle my thoughts of anger and help me to leave them in the past. Help me to pass on the grace that You have given me. Amen.

Too Much Talking

It's no secret that girls love to talk. And often they like to talk about their problems. It feels good to have the support of friends.

But there is danger in too much talking. Experts found that when girls rehashed their problems over and over again, they were more likely to get depressed and anxious. And being with a friend who was always dwelling on the negative brought all of her friends down too.

So instead of simply repeating the same negative conversation over and over, discuss a problem and ask your friends to help you come up with some possible solutions. You can still have the support of your friends, but the problem will shrink instead of grow.[19]

The BIG Ones

Some problems are just too big to tackle on your own. If someone has bullied or abused you or if you find yourself depressed about a problem, don't keep it to yourself. Please get help. Talk to a parent, your pastor, your youth counselor, or your school counselor.

Don't think you have to fix things on your own. There are people who care about you.

Day Five
Wardrobe Workout

1. Do you agree that too much talking about a problem can make it worse? Why or why not?

2. How do you and your friends discuss problems? Do you tend to constantly rehash them? Or do you brainstorm solutions too?

3. What do these verses tell us about handling problems with people?

   a. Proverbs 16:28

   b. Proverbs 17:9

   c. Proverbs 17:27

4. Get a close-up. Zoom in on one thing you discovered today.

5. Write out Ephesians 4:32 from memory.

Meaningful Makeover

Is there someone you need to forgive? Perhaps when you read that question, a face immediately appeared in your mind. If not, take a few minutes to ask God to show you if there is any bitterness or anger in your heart. Let Him show you if there is someone you need to forgive.

Use the steps for forgiveness that we outlined on Day 4:

1. Pray. Ask God to help you forgive. We can't do it on our own.

2. Write on a piece of paper what the other person did to you. Now look at what you wrote and tell God, "Lord, I forgive _____ for _____."

3. Destroy the piece of paper. Rip it into tiny pieces, put it through the shredder, burn it in the fireplace—anything to symbolize that you are no longer holding on to that hurt.

4. Take the next step. If the other person has asked for forgiveness or has said she is sorry, go to her and let her know that you have forgiven her. But if she isn't really sorry for the pain she caused or isn't even aware that she has done something hurtful, you probably won't want to confront her. It might make matters worse. But you could write a letter—a letter you won't send—telling her you have forgiven her for the hurt she brought to your life. Even if it is for your eyes only, it will help you feel like you have shut the door on that hurt.

Remind yourself that you are not forgiving the other person because she deserves it. You are offering forgiveness because Christ has given it to you. You are releasing your anger because it is caging your spirit. Forgiveness sets your soul free.

Remember to bring your sweater to your group's meeting!

Fashion
Finesse

A few words about finding the right clothes, building
a wardrobe, and looking your best.

The Shape of Sweaters

Sweaters come in a zillion shapes and styles. God created us in all
shapes and sizes. How do you choose the one that looks best on you?

The key is to create balance and proportion. Here are a few guidelines
for choosing sweaters that will make you look fabulous.

If your shape is:	Use these guidelines:	And try these styles:
Hourglass Evenly proportioned, small waist	Emphasize your waist, choose a style that skims your body, nothing too baggy	Wrap sweaters, belted sweaters
Triangle Smaller on the top, larger on the bottom	Draw attention to your upper body with the details at the neck or shoulders, wear bulky or thick knit sweaters, choose styles that end near your waist	Cowl-neck sweaters, boatneck sweaters, thick turtleneck sweaters, ruffled styles
Inverted triangle Larger on the top, smaller on the bottom	Wear lightweight sweaters, look for looser fit, wear V-neck styles	V-neck cardigans and pullovers
Rectangle Pretty much straight up and down	Choose bulky knits, styles that create a waist with a belt, or horizontal stripes	Wrap sweaters, belted cardigans, cable knits

God created us in all shapes and sizes. We can use fashion to
make the most of the shape we've been given. Every shape is
beautiful in its own way!

WEEK EIGHT

Look in the Mirror and See a New You

Memory Verse

And we all, who with unveiled faces contemplate the Lord's glory, are being transformed into His image with ever-increasing glory, which comes from the Lord, who is the Spirit.

2 Corinthians 3:18 (NIV)

Day One

Defective Mirrors

I praise You, for I am fearfully and wonderfully made.
Wonderful are Your works; my soul knows it very well.
Psalm 139:14

Welcome to the last week of our Divine Makeover! We've ditched the commander's uniform, the heavy handbag of worry, and the prom dress of pride. Envy-green outfits, boots of selfishness, and bitterness sweaters are in the trash. It's time to look in the mirror and see how we've changed.

But wait—we have to look in the right mirror. Otherwise we might be seeing the counterfeit reflections the world displays. Like the distorted glass in a funhouse, those images constantly try to tell us that we don't measure up.

The cover of *Shape* magazine yells "Loser!" because I'm not as fit as the model in the photo. The Neutrogena commercial screams "Ugly!" because my skin isn't flawless. The Macy's ad shouts "Failure!" because I can't afford those designer jeans.

Too often we believe these messages even though they're lies. We base our self-worth on impossible beauty standards. We compare ourselves with Photoshopped images that portray women the size of breadsticks. We look in the defective mirrors of our culture and wonder why we feel so bad about ourselves.

I know a young woman, now in her twenties, who lost herself for a while because she saw her reflection in some of these defective mirrors. Listen to Katherine tell her story:

> I've always been tall for my age. In fact, by the time I was
> about twelve, I had reached my full adult height and had
> started to develop some curves. But instead of seeing this
> as a blessing, I just saw that I had gained a few pounds and
> some of my clothes weren't fitting like they used to. Most of

my friends were thin, and I started to compare myself with
them and see myself as fat, even though I definitely wasn't.

Shortly after I began "filling out," I got a bad case of bron-
chitis that lasted a month or two. I lost all of the weight
I had gained and a little more. Then several people com-
mented that I had lost weight. I'm not sure if they meant it
as a compliment or a concern, but at the time, I took it as
a compliment and decided that if losing a little weight was
good, then losing more would be better.

This started the year when food consumed my thoughts and
life. Whenever I looked in the mirror, all I saw were im-
perfections. I constantly thought about what I "could" and
"couldn't" eat so I could lose more weight. My parents were
concerned about me, but for a long time I couldn't see that
anything was wrong. I was blinded by lies.

* * * * * * *

Okay, girls, can you agree that it's time to stop looking in the mirrors
that the media is holding up? It's time to stop listening to Satan's lies that
you aren't good enough, not thin enough, not beautiful enough. It's time to
look in God's mirror—His Word.

Only God's mirror will give you an accurate picture of yourself. Only
God's mirror will tell you the truth—that you are fearfully and wonderfully
made.

Read again what King David said in Psalm 139:14:

I praise You, for I am fearfully and wonderfully made.
Wonderful are your works; my soul knows it very well.

That word *fearfully* doesn't mean you are afraid to look at your reflection. It means "to be in awe of." David is saying, "Lord, I praise You because
You made me in a wonderful and awesome way!" God's mirror—His Word—
says that He used His awesome power to make you, and He has a wonderful plan for your life. When Katherine began looking at God's mirror, she
realized that all of the other mirrors she had been looking at were deceiving.

Her story has a happy ending:

> Eventually, I began to recognize that I had issues to deal
> with if I wanted to really live again. God showed me that
> my life had become consumed with food. I was spending all
> of my time thinking about food and my body and not about
> Him. My body and food had become my idols, instead of a
> temple of the Holy Spirit and nourishment for it. Slowly, I
> gave up the lies and started to live freely again. Now I could
> think about other areas of my life. I could think about what
> God wanted me to do with the life He gave me.
>
> The process of choosing to see myself as God sees me and
> not believe the false lies of a pretend mirror began my jour-
> ney of letting go of an unhealthy amount of control of my
> life and allowing God to mold me into the person He wants
> me to be.

* * * * * * *

Katherine is now a lovely, healthy young woman, living a life of service
to others. Her beauty in Christ shines out to the people around her.

Learn to look at God's mirror as Katherine did. Ask Him to help you
see yourself as He sees you—beautiful and whole in Christ. When Satan tries
to get you to believe His lies, repeat the words of Psalm 139: "I am fearfully
and wonderfully made." When the world holds up another deceptive mirror,
believe God's truth: He loves you just as you are.

> *Heavenly Father, sometimes it's hard for me to like*
> *myself. When I look at beautiful pictures of other girls, I*
> *feel like I don't measure up. Help me to reject all those*
> *distorted images and look at the truth of Your Word: I am*
> *wonderfully made. In Jesus' name. Amen.*

Avoiding the Defective Mirrors

What can you do when the world holds up distorted mirrors? What can you do when you find yourself believing their lies? Here are a few practical tips to help you focus on the truth.

1. Write a list of things you can do with your body: play the piano, ice-skate, bake cookies, and so forth. See if you can list a hundred abilities.

2. Avoid magazines or media that present unhealthy body images.

3. Oscar Wilde said, "Be yourself; everyone else is already taken." Post this quote on your mirror and remember that you are a beautiful, one-of-a-kind daughter of God.

4. Tell a friend what you like most about her looks, her personality. Then ask her to do the same for you.

5. Write Psalm 139:14 on a sticky note and carry it around with you in your purse or backpack.

Day One
Wardrobe Workout

1. What are some of the defective mirrors you see around you? What ads or images sometimes make you dislike your looks?

2. Write down ten things that your body can do. This will help you concentrate on the health and abilities of your body and focus less on its
   appearance.

a. _____   f. _____
   _____   _____
   _____   _____
   _____   _____
   _____   _____

b. _____   g. _____
   _____   _____
   _____   _____
   _____   _____
   _____   _____

c. _____   h. _____
   _____   _____
   _____   _____
   _____   _____
   _____   _____

d. _____   i. _____
   _____   _____
   _____   _____
   _____   _____
   _____   _____

e. _____   j. _____
   _____   _____
   _____   _____
   _____   _____
   _____   _____

3. If you are doing this in a group, take some time to share what you like about the other people in your group. You can do this in a circle with everyone or in pairs.

4. Read Psalm 139:13–16.

   a. A healthy body image begins with respect for the way God made you. How does this psalm honor God's creation?

   b. Is it difficult for you to say "I am fearfully and wonderfully made"? Why or why not?

   c. Write your own mini-psalm using some of David's words and the list you wrote in question 2 above.

   Lord, I praise you because You have given me the ability to:

5. Get a close-up. Zoom in on one thing you discovered today.

6. Our memory verse for this week is 2 Corinthians 3:18: "And we all, who with unveiled faces contemplate the Lord's glory, are being transformed into His image with ever-increasing glory, which comes from the Lord, who is the Spirit" (NIV). To help you memorize this passage, write it out on several sticky notes and post them on mirrors in your house. Also, write it out in the space below.

Day Two

◇◇◇◇◇◇◇◇◇◇◇◇◇◇◇◇◇◇◇◇

Beautiful Hearts

For the LORD *sees not as man sees: man looks on the out-*
ward appearance, but the LORD *looks on the heart.*
1 Samuel 16:7

Marissa was hanging out with a few friends at a sleepover when she first noticed it. She pulled her long blond hair into a ponytail and there it was—a small bald patch about the size of a quarter at the back of her head.

Marissa panicked. She had just watched a television show about alopecia—a show where people who were totally *bald (!)* talked about that condition. Marissa immediately called her mom and told her she thought she had alopecia. Her mom laughed it off and told her not to worry.

They went to a dermatologist a few days later. He gave Marissa an injection of a steroid and her hair grew back. Small bald patches appeared several more times, but the injections seemed to take care of the problem.

Then Marissa went through a bad breakup with a boyfriend and suddenly noticed a bald spot the size of a baseball! The doctors told her stress was causing her hair loss and they couldn't do anything to help. Her hair began falling out in clumps. Marissa had to get a wig.

Eventually Marissa lost all of her hair on her head, arms, and legs—even her eyebrows and eyelashes. It turned out she did indeed have alopecia. In fact, she had *alopecia universalis*—the worst form of the condition.

As Marissa's hair fell out, her self-esteem took a nosedive. After all, in our culture, shiny, healthy hair is a big part of a beautiful image. Marissa wondered if her friends would accept her without hair. She thought surely no guy would ever want a bald woman.

Why was God allowing this to happen? Marissa's faith was shaken. Gradually, she began to accept her condition. When she asked her dad to shave off the last few strands of hair on her head, it never grew back. She thought, *Obviously, God wants me to go through this. Worry and stress are what got me into this. More worry is not going to make things better.*

207

Eventually, Marissa saw that alopecia had changed who she was. What she looked like was no longer her number one priority. She didn't spend hours worrying about her appearance.

What other people looked like became less important too. She stopped judging others by their appearance and realized that everyone has a story that you can't always see.

Now in her twenties, Marissa is working on a master's degree in social work. Her experience with alopecia has inspired her to help people with their inner struggles. She speaks to teens who are wrestling with self-esteem issues. Marissa wants every girl to know that she can be loved and liked no matter what she looks like.

Just to let you know, Marissa is gorgeous. She is beautiful inside and out. Last year, she married a cute guy who loves her for who she is and not for what she looks like.

Marissa's experience reminds me of what the Bible says about our outward appearance:

> For the LORD sees not as man sees: man looks on the
> outward appearance, but the LORD looks on the heart.
> 1 Samuel 16:7

God sees your beauty. He's looking at your gorgeous heart. He loves you just as you are. And He doesn't want you to be so caught up with what you look like on the outside. He wants you to focus on your inner beauty.

Like Marissa, we can all learn to accept ourselves as the Father made us and see the beauty there. We can grow in faith and start to accept our problems as ways God is changing us into the people He wants us to be.

And when we see ourselves through God's eyes, we can also learn to stop judging others by their appearance. We realize that everyone has their own troubles, their own stories. We don't accept them for their looks alone. We see their beautiful hearts.

> *Heavenly Father, thank You that You have made my*
> *heart beautiful. Help me not to focus on my outward ap-*
> *pearance or judge others by how they look. Like You, help*
> *me to see their hearts. In Jesus' name. Amen.*

Beautiful Hearts

God's Word tells us that in Christ, our hearts are beautiful. Here are some examples of lovely hearts:

- Hearts full of God's words: Deuteronomy 11:18

- Hearts that trust: John 14:1

- Hearts controlled by God's peace: Colossians 3:15

- Hearts full of gratitude: Colossians 3:16

- Hearts that are pure: James 4:8

Day Two
Wardrobe Workout

1. Do you believe Marissa's statement that every girl can be loved and liked no matter what she looks like? Why or why not?

2. The Bible has a lot to say about our beautiful hearts. The sidebar above has some examples. Here are a few more. Look up these passages and write down the characteristic of a beautiful heart that you see there.

   1 Kings 8:61 _____

   Mark 11:23 _____

   Romans 5:5 _____

   Galatians 4:6 _____

3. Get a close-up. Zoom in on one thing you discovered today.

4. Write out our memory verse for this week: "And we all, who with un-veiled faces contemplate the Lord's glory, are being transformed into His image with ever-increasing glory, which comes from the Lord, who is the Spirit" (2 Corinthians 3:18 NIV). Read a phrase, then cover it and write it. Try to write as much of the verse as you can without looking.

Day Three
◇◇◇◇◇◇◇◇◇◇◇◇◇◇◇◇◇◇◇◇◇◇
She's Got the Look

For in Christ Jesus you are all sons of God, through faith.
For as many of you as were baptized into Christ have put
on Christ. Galatians 3:26–27

I took a step back and looked at the bride. She was radiant in her white gown. A smile lit her face when she saw her reflection in the mirrors all around the room. Her beauty was obvious.

During my college years, I worked at a bridal salon each summer. I got to work with stunning bridal gowns, lovely bridesmaids' dresses, and gor-geous formals. I could run my fingers over smooth satin and intricate lace. I was able to see the latest designs covered with sequins and pearls. Each dress was a work of art.

What made the job especially interesting was watching the transforma-tion in the girls who came in to try on the dresses. Since it was summertime, most of them came into the store wearing shorts, flip-flops, and a T-shirt. Not particularly glamorous.

When a girl arrived for her fitting, I showed her to a room covered with mirrors and brought in her dress. I slipped the dress over her head. From the smiles visible in every mirror, I could tell that she suddenly felt like a princess. In just a few minutes, she was transformed from an ordinary girl in summer shorts to a dazzling beauty in a stunning gown.

The Holy Spirit does something like that for us in our hearts. Because of Adam and Eve's sin, we are born with dirty hearts. We are hopeless and helpless. But when we first receive the gift of faith, the Holy Spirit begins our divine makeover. He starts by clothing us in Christ. Galatians 3:26–27 says:

> For in Christ Jesus you are all sons of God, through faith.
> For as many of you as were baptized into Christ have put
> on Christ.

What does it mean to "put on Christ"? When we put on clothes, they cover our bodies. When people look at us, they see the outfit, not our skin. When we put on Christ, He is the one that others see. In God's eyes, we are no longer ordinary girls—we are princesses in His kingdom. We are radically changed.

When a girl came into the bridal salon for her fitting, it was very rare that the dress fit her perfectly. Yes, she was instantly transformed when I slipped the white satin over her head. She looked beautiful. But usually the dress needed a bit of work. Perhaps I would need to shorten the dress an inch. Or nip it in at the waist. Or let out a seam or two. I didn't stop until the dress fit perfectly.

The Holy Spirit does the same for our spirits. Once we have received Christ, we are spectacularly changed. In Baptism, we are clothed with Christ and He covers all of our mistakes and sins. We are beautiful in God's eyes.

But while we are still on earth, we're not perfect. So the Holy Spirit keeps on working. He alters our hearts by giving us faith and trust and hope. He shows us where we need to make a few adjustments, and He offers forgiveness at the Lord's Table. He gives us the desire to look more and more like Christ.

When I altered a wedding dress, there were two possibilities: (1) either I needed to subtract a bit of the dress—shorten the skirt or take in the waist; or (2) I had to add something to the dress—let out the side seams or add a bit of lace to the neckline. When the Holy Spirit works in our lives, He often needs to subtract something from or add something to our lives.

Ask the Spirit to show you if there is something in your life that needs to be removed.

Do you need to subtract
- a particular TV show?
- friends that aren't the best influences in your life?
- hidden sins?
- teen magazines that only make you feel bad about yourself?
- trying to be perfect?

Or is the Holy Spirit working to help you add something to your life to bring you closer to God?

Do you need to add
- more time in God's Word?
- a more-consistent prayer life?
- trust in God's goodness?
- confidence that comes from God's immense love for you?
- friends who love the Lord?

Let the Holy Spirit work. He will alter your spirit, making it even more beautiful. With each addition or subtraction, you will become more Christ-like. You will have the look—the look of Christ.

"Putting on Christ" is not just playing dress-up. The Holy Spirit changes us from the inside out. A beautiful gown may make you *look* like a princess, but when you are clothed with Christ, you truly *are* a princess—a daughter of the King.

> *Dear Holy Spirit, now I know the image You want me to have—the image of Christ. Change me from the inside out. Show me what needs to be added or subtracted in my life to make me more like Jesus. Amen.*

Adding On

Just as a seamstress may have to add something to a dress to make it more beautiful, sometimes the Holy Spirit works to add character to our souls to make us more Christlike. 2 Peter 1:5–7 has a list of things to add to our lives:

faith

virtue

knowledge

self-control

steadfastness

godliness

affection

love

Day Three
Wardrobe Workout

1. Look at the list of things to add and subtract from our lives. Can you think of any other things to put on those lists?

   a. Subtract:

   b. Add:

c. Take a minute to ask the Holy Spirit to show you what He wants you to add or subtract from your life. Write a short prayer below asking for His help in carrying that out.

2. Galatians 3:26–27 says that we have "put on Christ." As we grow in faith, we will look more and more like Jesus. To discover more about what it means to look like Jesus, look up the following passages and write down some of His characteristics.

   a. Matthew 9:36: Example: Jesus was compassionate.

   b. Matthew 11:29: _____

   c. Mark 10:45: _____

   d. Luke 23:34: _____

3. Get a close-up. Zoom in on one thing you discovered today.

4. Write out this week's memory verse. Try to do it without looking back at the words.

Day Four

◇◇◇◇◇◇◇◇◇◇◇◇◇◇◇◇◇◇◇◇

Your Mirror, Lord

*And we all, who with unveiled faces contemplate the
Lord's glory, are being transformed into His image with
ever-increasing glory, which comes from the Lord, who is
the Spirit. 2 Corinthians 3:18 (NIV)*

One warm, sunny day my friend James was hiking in the Black Hills of
South Dakota. He discovered a large piece of mica on the ground and picked
it up. He turned it over and marveled at its many thin, glasslike layers. The
rock looked dusty and dirty, nothing special. But when he tried to brush off
some of the dirt, some of the thin layers broke away, and suddenly the rock
shone in the sunlight. James suspected that there was something beautiful
under all that dirt, so he flaked off more of the dusty pieces. With each layer
that he peeled off, the rock got shinier. Each layer became clearer. Removing
the dirt revealed a surface that had been hidden deep in the rock but now
shone as brilliantly as a mirror.

James told me this story because he said the beauty of the rock reminded him of life in Christ. We all start out like the dirty mica—our spirits
don't look like much. The beauty of our souls is buried under a lot of ugly
stuff. But God patiently waits for us to come to Him so He can peel away all
the dirty layers and make us shine. He takes away our selfishness, worry, and
pride and reveals our true beauty in Christ. He gently removes our envy and
bitterness so we can reflect Jesus.

My friend James was so inspired by this little piece of mica that he
wrote a song called "Mirror." And because James was a part of that group
of musicians I traveled with in Miracle White (remember the story on page
69–71?), I had the privilege of singing that song. Out of all the songs we

performed that year, "Mirror" was my favorite. The words express what I
want my life to be:

I long to be Your mirror, Lord
I pray that You will be
the one who will be noticed
when people look at me.
They'll see You . . . Jesus.[20]

More than anything, I want my life to be a reflection of Jesus. I want
people to look at me and see the image of Christ. I want to mirror Jesus'
love to the people around me.

The apostle Paul also talked being transformed into Christ's image:

> And we all, who with unveiled faces contemplate the Lord's
> glory, are being transformed into His image with ever-
> increasing glory, which comes from the Lord, who is the
> Spirit. 2 Corinthians 3:18 (NIV)

Sometimes I beat myself up because although I have known Jesus for
a long time, I feel that I don't do a very good job of reflecting His image to
others. When people see me, do they see Jesus?

That's why I love this verse. It says we are *being* transformed into
Christ's image. I'm not there yet. My transformation won't be complete until I'm in heaven. But God is continuously changing me. Little by little, the
Holy Spirit is peeling away all the stuff that prevents me from being a clear
reflection of God's love. Every day He removes a little more of the dirt from
my image.

And while the Holy Spirit is working, I am learning to look at Jesus.
After all, I can only reflect Him when I am looking at Him. When I gaze
steadily at Christ, I grow closer to Him. I begin to know Him better. I start
to mirror His character.

Do you long to be a mirror of the Lord? Allow Him to peel away the
layers that are preventing your true self from shining. Look into Jesus' face
and reflect His love to the world.

> *Dear Lord, I do long to be Your mirror. I pray that when*
> *people look at me, all they see is You. Peel away any lay-*
> *ers of my old self that are getting in the way of reflecting*
> *Your grace. Amen.*

A Makeup Prayer

While you are looking in the mirror to put on your makeup, try adding prayer to your routine.

While you put on:	Pray for:
moisturizer	God to soothe your soul.
mascara	eyes to see others as Christ sees them.
concealer	Jesus to cover over your sins.
lip gloss	the ability to speak encouraging words.

Day Four

◇◇◇◇◇◇◇◇◇◇◇◇◇◇◇◇◇◇◇◇◇◇

Wardrobe Workout

1. How are our lives here on earth like the piece of mica that my friend James found?

2. Read 2 Corinthians 3:18. This verse tells us we are being transformed into Christ's image. It's a continual process. Think back in your life a bit. How has God transformed you from what you were before? Do see changes in your character?

3. Get a close-up. Zoom in on one thing you discovered today.

4. Write out the memory verse for this week. No peeking!

217

Study Styles
Studying a Bible Character

The Bible is full of interesting stories about people. People who loved God and people who didn't. People who won and people who lost. People who lived good lives and people who totally messed up.

We can learn a lot by studying the lives of some of these people. When we read their stories, we can discover the good things about them and try to copy those good qualities. We can learn about their mistakes and try to avoid them.

We are going to do a mini-study of Esther. She was a young woman who lived in Persia (now Iran) around 400 BC. Because there's a whole book of the Bible written about her, we could spend months studying her life, but we are going to concentrate on just a few characteristics of this interesting woman who was probably about your age when God called her for a special mission.

Step 1: Read about the person you are studying.

Read the story of Esther in the Bible. If you don't have time to read all ten chapters, read this summary of the beginning of the story.

Summary: As the book opens, Esther is a young Jewish woman living in the kingdom of Persia. The Jewish people are foreigners in the land, brought there by a king long ago. The current ruler, King Xerxes (Ahasuerus), is looking for a new wife and holds a sort of beauty pageant to pick a new queen. Esther is chosen to be the new queen and lives in the palace, but life does not continue happily ever after. One of the king's advisors becomes obsessed with anger at the Jews and asks King Xerxes to order the killing of the Jews throughout the country. Mordecai, Esther's cousin and adoptive father, secretly contacts Esther and asks her to go to the king to ask for mercy for the Jews.

Now read:
Esther 4
Esther 5:1–7
Esther 7
Esther 8:1–8

Step 2: Look for character qualities of the person you are studying.

As you read, look for Esther's character qualities. What stands out about her personality? What would make you like her? Is there anything about her you didn't like?

Step 3: Tell how she showed this character quality.

How did Esther demonstrate that personality trait? For instance, if she was kind, how did she show kindness?

Step 4: Choose one verse that demonstrates that quality.

Pick one verse from what you read that best shows Esther living out that quality.

Step 5: Apply that quality to your life.

If the quality is a good quality, how can you build it into your life? If it is a bad trait, how can you get rid of it in your own character? Try to come up with one specific thing you can do this week. I have shared an example for you from Esther 2.

Character Quality	A Verse That Shows That Quality	How I Will Apply It to My Life This Week	How Esther Demonstrated that Quality
Wisdom	Esther 2:15	When my parents give me advice, I will listen because they have more experience than I do.	Esther followed the advice of the king's most trusted advisor

Day Five

◇◇◇◇◇◇◇◇◇◇◇◇◇

Mirror, Mirror

Therefore, if anyone is in Christ, he is a new creation.
The old has passed away; behold, the new has come.
2 Corinthians 5:17

"Mirror, mirror on the wall, who's the fairest of them all?" Do you remember those words spoken by the evil queen in the Snow White fairy tale? Every time the queen approached the mirror, she fully expected the mirror to reply, "You, O queen, are the fairest of them all." And watch out if this wasn't the answer she received! If the mirror mentioned anyone else, that poor girl was quickly done away with, so the next day, the evil queen could receive the reply she wanted from her mirror.

Who wouldn't want a mirror that gave a daily dose of compliments? We all long to be attractive and sought after. We all want to be told that we're beautiful.

The bathroom mirror might not always give us the answer we want when we ask ourselves the question, "Am I beautiful?" After all, bad hair days, bad skin days, bad *everything* days happen now and then.

But there is a mirror that will always tell us we are beautiful—in Christ. Because of Jesus' sacrifice for us, we always look lovely in God's looking glass. Our heavenly Father sees us not as we are, with our mammoth mistakes, our messy sins, our major bedhead. He sees us as we will be—perfect. The Bible tells us, "If anyone is in Christ, he is a new creation" (2 Corinthians 5:17).

In God's eyes, we're already beautiful because He sees us dressed in the robes of Christ's purity. He watches your makeover progress, but at the same time, He sees you in your final photo shoot. God can already envision "the big reveal."

When we have trouble seeing past the flawed image in our bathroom mirror, we need to look at God's mirror—His Word. In it, God tells us over and over how much He loves us. When media, self-doubt, or even my friends leave me feeling unloved and unlovely, I can look in God's miraculous mirror to see who I am in His eyes.

In His Word, God tells me I am:

beautiful

You are altogether beautiful, my love; there is no flaw in you. Song of Solomon 4:7

Wow! Because of Jesus, when God looks at me, He sees me as perfect.

where He finds joy

But the LORD takes pleasure in those who fear Him, in those who hope in His steadfast love. Psalm 147:11

Amazing! I make God happy.

His bride

As the bridegroom rejoices over the bride, so shall your God rejoice over you. Isaiah 62:5

God sees me as a lovely, pure bride.

a reason to sing

The LORD your God is in your midst, a mighty one who will save; He will rejoice over you with gladness; He will quiet you by His love; He will exult over you with loud singing. Zephaniah 3:17

Imagine! God is singing songs about me! He's looking down from heaven with love.

precious and honored

Because you are precious in My eyes, and honored, and I love you, I give men in return for you, peoples in exchange for your life. Isaiah 43:4

I am important to God. I am so precious to Him that He exchanged His Son's life for mine.

lavished with love

See what great love the Father has lavished on us, that we should be called children of God! And that is what we are! (1 John 3:1 NIV)

God doesn't carefully give a tiny spoonful of love. He lavishes love on me!

So on days when you doubt your beauty, look in God's mirror. When you're feeling insignificant, remember that you are precious to God. When it feels like no one loves you, repeat the words, "How great is the love the Father has lavished on me."

Girls, when you know in your heart that you're loved like that, you can trust the One who loves you. You can believe that God really does know what He is doing when He is peeling away the grime from your lives, even though the process might be a little painful.

Let God take control. Give Him your worries. Throw away the prom dress of pride and learn to wear humility. Forget about wearing envy green, and allow Christ to dress you in contentment. Give up on selfishness and put on the shoes of love and sacrifice. Let Jesus unravel your bitterness and give you His grace to forgive.

Your divine makeover won't be complete until you see Jesus face to face. But even now you are perfect in God's eyes. Even now you are made new.

> *Dear Father, I'm so glad that You don't only see me as I am now. I love that You also see me as I will be—perfect in Christ. Please keep working a divine makeover in my heart. In Jesus' name. Amen.*

Mirror, Mirror

Make a copy (or three!) of the chart on page 221 of how God sees you. Post it on your mirror to remind you that even on your bad hair days, in God's eyes you are incredible! Put one in your locker, by your computer, in your purse. Look at it whenever you need to hear God's mirror telling you that you are beautiful!

Day Five
Wardrobe Workout

1. What is your reaction to the following words? "Our heavenly Father sees us not as we are with our mammoth mistakes, our messy sins, our major bedhead. He sees us as we will be—perfect."

2. Look again at the chart on page 221. Which verse means the most to you? Why?

3. Get a close-up. Zoom in on one thing you discovered today.

4. Write out 2 Corinthians 3:18 from memory.

Meaningful Makeover

Think back over our whole makeover process. In cleaning out our closets, we've tossed out some ugly attitudes and made room for more Christlike beauty.

We have exchanged the: for:

uniform of control   surrender and acceptance

handbag of worry   trust

prom dress of pride   humility

green of envy   contentment

boots of selfishness   love

sweater of bitterness   forgiveness

Where have you seen the biggest change? In which area was your makeover most dramatic?

Which area still needs work?

Don't worry. Our divine makeover won't be complete until we get to heaven. But the Holy Spirit will continue to work wonders in our spirits. He gently removes the things that mess up our image and gives us new items to help us shine.

Congratulations on finishing our forty-day makeover! I wish I could take a picture of your beautiful heart and display it to the world. I wish the networks would air the show *Extreme Makeover: Heart Edition* so that everyone could see the miracle makeover God has worked in your spirit. Spend a little time thanking God for His love and grace that has transformed you.

If you'd like to continue your divine makeover, I have a little challenge for you. Take this forty-day challenge to continue your adventure in God's Word:

- For the next forty days, spend fifteen minutes each day reading the Bible.
- Each day, write down a word of grace—how God sees you in Christ.
- Every day, find a word of transformation—where God wants you to change.
- Sign this challenge (see page 226).

* * * * * * *

As I finish writing this book, I'm praying for you. Praying that you will see yourself as a deeply loved daughter of the King. Praying that on the days when you don't like what you see in the mirror, you will believe God's words to you, "You are altogether beautiful, My love" (Song of Solomon 4:7). Praying that the beauty of your heart will shine out to everyone you meet.

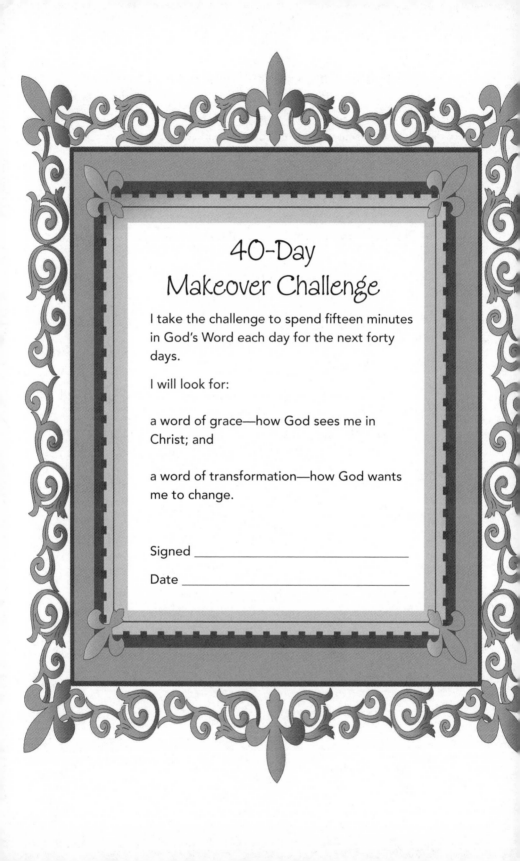

40-Day
Makeover Challenge

I take the challenge to spend fifteen minutes in God's Word each day for the next forty days.

I will look for:

a word of grace—how God sees me in Christ; and

a word of transformation—how God wants me to change.

Signed _____

Date _____

A few words about finding the right clothes, building a wardrobe, and looking your best.

Faith and Fashion—Putting It All Together

How do faith and fashion connect? In our Divine Makeover, we've spent a lot of time discussing inner beauty. We've talked a little about making fashion choices. How do the two topics intersect?

1. **What you wear communicates who you are.** Let your personal style come through. Lori is totally okay with wearing T-shirts and jeans whenever she can. Brittany likes to experiment with the latest trends. Don't feel like you have to dress like someone else. Over time, you will discover which clothes fit your body and personality best.

2. **What you wear represents Christ.** Did you ever think that when people look at you, they are looking at Jesus? What we choose to put on our bodies can affect the way others see God.

   Because God gives us instructions to dress modestly, we want our clothing to reflect our honor for God's gift of sexuality. When we dress in cute clothes that still cover up all the important parts, we are communicating that we're fun, but we intend to live God's way.

3. **What you wear can change how you see yourself—and others.** We've spent most of this book talking about our inner beauty. And that's the way it should be. More of our time should be spent in God's Word than in front of the mirror.

But I have found that when I feel comfortable in what I'm wearing, I begin to forget about myself. When I feel I look my best, I have a confidence that helps me silence all those nagging thoughts in my head: *Do I look okay? What are they thinking about me?* When those thoughts are quiet, I am much more able to think about others. I am free to concentrate on what the other person is saying and care about their problems. So dress in a way that makes you feel confident enough to forget about yourself and focus on others.

Remember that you are beautiful. God made you in a special and unique way. Don't try to be someone else. You are a spectacular one-of-a-kind.

Extras

◇◇◇◇◇◇◇◇◇◇◇◇◇◇◇◇◇◇◇◇◇◇◇◇

Brand-New Clothes

God wants everyone to wear the brand-new clothes of salvation. Jesus, His Son, already purchased a robe of righteousness just for you. He paid the price through His perfect life, death, and resurrection. When the Holy Spirit empowers you to believe that Jesus died and rose again for you, He gives you that beautiful garment of salvation.

God loves you and has a plan for you to know Him. He tells us this plan in the Bible, His Word to us.

- "For all have sinned and fall short of the glory of God" (Romans 3:23). No one is perfect. Everyone fails to meet God's standard of sinlessness. This sin prevents us from coming to Him and from entering heaven.
- "For God so loved the world, that He gave His only Son, that whoever believes in Him should not perish but have eternal life" (John 3:16). God loved us so much that He sent His own Son to take the punishment we deserved for our sins and mistakes. Jesus' death enables us to live with God—forever.
- "For by grace you have been saved through faith. And this is not your own doing; it is the gift of God" (Ephesians 2:8). God gives us faith to believe in Jesus. His grace and mercy save us from death.
- "But to all who did receive Him, who believed in His name, He gave the right to become children of God" (John 1:12). Through believing in Jesus, we become part of God's family.

I invite you to pray this prayer to the God who loves you and wants you to be part of His family:

> *Father in heaven, I realize that I am a sinner. I have messed up and have fallen short of what You want for my life. I know that I can't save myself or earn eternal life. Thank You for sending Your Son, Jesus, to die for me. Because He rose from the dead, You have also made me alive. Help me to turn from my sins and follow You.*

Thank You that although I may still fail, You will forgive
me because Jesus paid the price for my sins. Thank You
for Your gift of faith in Jesus, my Savior, and for the prom-
ise of eternal life with You. In Jesus' name I pray. Amen.

Through God's free gift of faith in Jesus, you now possess the garment of salvation. You have the robe of righteousness and life forever with God. He has begun your divine makeover!

What If I Don't Have Good Parents?

One week I was discussing the issue of honoring parents with a group of teenage girls. All the girls agreed that most parents want the best for their kids. Even though parents aren't perfect, they truly are trying to be the most loving and caring providers for their children. But one girl in our group asked, "What if someone doesn't have good parents? What do they do with the instructions to honor and obey them?"

I hope that none of you reading this book is in that situation, but just in case some of you are, I asked two experts to help me answer that question. My own husband, Pastor John Fritz, grew up in a home where it was very hard to honor his father. He answered the question from his own experience:

As the child of an alcoholic who downed a quart of brandy every day in his last months, I've had some practice in trying to honor the parents God gave me while hating their sinful behaviors. My parents got the first divorce on our block while I was starting high school. It was nasty and extremely stressful for our whole family. Mom tried to make sure that we would see Dad for holidays, but would not provide liquor for him, and we were too young to legally buy it even if we wanted to. This would lead to his loudly disowning us on Christmas and even our birthdays. Money problems, rage, cursing, insults, stepfamilies, an alleged attempted stabbing, and Dad wistfully talking about shooting my sister's boyfriend added up to dysfunction with a deadly capital D!

Even with all the toxic transgressions spewing around me and the trips to see Dad in the detox ward, I made the effort to try to respect honorable aspects of my earthly father's life while hating his alcohol-fueled descent, irrational ranting, and his attacks against my mom and sister. He did teach me the value of hard work, a twisted sort of rugged individualism, and, by negative example, the value of an intact family, and the horrors of chemical dependency.

My husband did his best to honor his father where he could while hating his father's sinful behaviors. Although my husband did not have a perfect childhood, God used all of those experiences. Because John knows what it is to hurt, he has become a very caring, loving person.

Micah Steiner is director of Christian education at Our Father Lutheran Church in Centennial, Colorado. He shares his answer to the question "What if I don't have good parents?" from his experience of working with teenagers and families:

I'll admit, honoring an authority figure, especially a parent, who is mean, uncaring, unloving, distant, angry, can be very difficult. Oftentimes we struggle showing them love or respect because the things they say (or don't say) leave us frustrated or angry ourselves. Yet, despite the way this makes us feel, we are still asked by God to honor our parents (and authority figures). So a better question to ask ourselves is, "How can I honor my parents when they don't behave appropriately?" A few suggestions:

1. Seek out a trusted Christian adult (pastor, youth leader, teacher, etc.) who will challenge you to live a life of authenticity and integrity. Find someone who will encourage you in your faith, provide a listening ear when you grow frustrated with your parents, and provide prayer support when you feel like you just want to give up. He or she can't replace your parents, but can provide some consistency in your life when you really need it.

2. Spend a lot of time in prayer! Only God has the power to change hearts and minds, including yours. Ask Him for help and strength!

3. Meditate on God's word. Let's be honest with ourselves . . . we don't want to show honor to someone who doesn't honor us! If it's going to happen, we will need God's supernatural presence in our lives, and one of the ways that happens is by studying His love letter to us. Here are a few verses to get you started: Psalm 139; Romans 12:9–21; Matthew 11:27–29.

4. Worship. Ask God to reveal His goodness to you and change your heart so that you can let go of all bitterness and instead, live a life that partners with God and brings good into a dark and broken world. The best place for this change to happen in your heart is in worship, where you experience the Sacraments (God's real and good presence in your body!) and where you are surrounded by God's saints, who are there to encourage you in your walk of faith.

I pray that you will find the love and help you need from the only perfect Parent, our heavenly Father, and from other trusted friends and adults who will build you up.

Attention: If one of your parent's behaviors actually falls into the **dangerously** sinful category, tell someone in authority for your own well-being and protection. If you are experiencing emotional, physical, or sexual abuse, get help from your other parent or a trusted aunt, uncle, or grandparent. Turn to a teacher, pastor, Christian counselor, social worker, or even the police. An abusive parent is breaking God's command to love his or her children and raise them up in a godly manner (see Ephesians 6:4). If you are being abused by a parent, this is clearly *not* God's command, and they are sinning against Him and you. Seek help from a trusted adult! (If you don't have an adult in your life you can trust, visit: www.thehotline.org.)

Setting Boundaries

Sexual passion can intensify quickly. If you don't set healthy boundaries, you may find yourself in a situation that you later regret. Live with integrity and guard your purity by establishing lines that you will not cross.

First establish boundary lines with your guy friends. Friends laugh together and talk with each other, but they don't try to turn each other on. Often girls do things with their bodies without realizing what their actions do to a guy's brain. Avoid close, body-touching hugs with your male friends. When you want to touch a guy friend, give his arm a squeeze, pat him on the back, or try the old side hug.

If you are in a dating relationship with a guy, remember that physical intimacy in a relationship can escalate quickly, so go slow. Establish a friendship first. Get to know the guy. When you begin to be more than friends, holding hands or walking arm in arm is appropriate.

As for kissing, some girls are choosing to save their kisses for their future spouse. If you decide this, tell your boyfriend of your intentions. But even if you decide to kiss before marriage, be aware that long, passionate kissing can be a surefire way to light up your sexual desire. It may lead to the temptation to go farther than you intended.

Establish the boundary of no touching private parts. Remember that you are being selfish with your body so you can give it to the man who takes the vow to love you for the rest of your life.

If at any time you start to feel warning bells go off in your head, saying, "This doesn't feel right," listen! Don't shut your ears when your heart is telling you to slow down. Simply smile and tell your boyfriend, "I prefer that you don't do that, okay?" If he respects you, he will listen.

God intends your sex life to be awesome—when the time is right. When you set up boundary lines and stick to them, you will be free to enjoy the beauty of sex with your husband on your wedding night and ever after. You will experience the gift of sexuality—without regrets.

◇◇◇◇◇◇◇◇◇◇◇◇◇◇◇◇◇◇◇◇◇◇◇◇◇◇
Study Guide Answers

Week One: Day One: 1. Answers will vary. 2. a. Answers will vary. b. Other possible desires include: desire for money, desire for power or control, desire for athletic ability, desire for friendship, desire for a boyfriend. c. Answers might include: love, patience, kindness, goodness, forgiving spirit, faithfulness, gentleness. 3. Answers will vary. 4. Memory verse. **Day Two:** 1. Answers will vary. 2. Answers will vary. 3. a. Answers will vary. b. The filthy garments picture our sin. c. The "pure vestments" symbolize God's gifts of salvation and forgiveness. d. God instructs an angel to take off Joshua's dirty clothes and put on clean ones. This symbolizes the fact that we cannot clean up our lives on our own; only God can do that. 4. Answers will vary. 5. Memory verse. **Day Three:** 1. Answers will vary. 2. Answers will vary. 3. a. Respectful and pure conduct. b. We can follow their example by doing what is right and not giving in to fear. c. An inner beauty regimen might include attending worship services, getting together with Christian friends for encouragement, personal Bible study, listening to Christian music, prayer, memorizing and meditating on Scripture. 4. Answers will vary. 5. Memory verse. **Day Four:** 1. Answers may vary but may include: We don't want to change. We are afraid to change. We try to change on our own instead of relying on God. 2. Modern-day idols may include money, success, fame, celebrities, nice clothes, looking good, career. 3. Answers will vary. 4. Memory verse. **Study Styles:** What Not to Wear: sexual immorality, impurity, passion, evil desire, covetousness, idolatry, anger, wrath, malice, slander, obscene talk, lying. What to Wear: compassionate hearts, kindness, humility, meekness, patience, forgiveness, love, peace of Christ, thankfulness. **Day Five:** 1. a. Answers will vary. b. Answers will vary. 2. Answers will vary. 3. a. Colossians 3:12 describes us as God's chosen ones, holy and beloved. b. Answers will vary but might include: Knowing that God loves me and has chosen me makes it easier to trust Him with my heart. 4. Answers will vary. 5. Memory verse. **Meaningful Makeover:** Answers will vary.

Week Two: Day One: 1. Answers will vary. 2. Answers will vary. 3. a. God promises peace and righteousness to those who follow His commands. b. Things will go better for us—"be well" with us—when we walk in God's ways and obey Him. c. We can show God that we love Him by obeying Him. His commands are not meant to be burdens. 4. Answers will vary. 5. Memory verse. **Day Two:** 1. Answers will vary. 2. a. Answers will vary but might include: Letting go of your idea of how your life should go. b. Answers will vary but might include: certain movies, books, or friends. It might include giving up free time to go to church and read God's Word. c. Answers will vary, but may include: When money or fame becomes our goal, we may compromise our values to get them. We might do things that we actually don't want to do, just to be popular. 3. Answers will vary. 4. Memory verse. **Day Three:** 1. Answers will vary. 2. Answers will vary but might include: Seeing myself as a daughter of the King helps me to do what God wants me to do, because a father wants what is best for his daughter and a king has unlimited riches that he wants to give to his daughter. 3. a. He wants us to wait patiently (v. 1). He wants us to praise Him (v. 3). He wants us to trust Him instead of other people (v. 4). He wants us to tell others what He has done for us (v. 5). He wants us to delight in His will—be happy to do what He wants (v. 8). He wants us to keep His law in our hearts (v. 8). b. Answers will vary. c. God hears our cries (v. 1). God gets us out of the pit (v. 2). God puts us on solid ground (v. 2). God puts a song in our mouths (v. 3). God blesses those who trust Him (v. 4). God performs amazing deeds for us (v. 5). d. Answers will vary. 4. Answers will vary. 5. Memory verse. **Day Four:** 1. Answers will vary. 2. a. Luke doesn't talk about the speck and the log. Luke mentions other positive actions: "forgive, and you will be forgiven; give, and it will be given to you." These verses promise that blessings will be given to you in the same way you give them. b. *judge, condemn, forgive, give.* c. Answers will vary. 3. Answers will vary. 4. Memory verse. **Study Styles:** Answers will vary. **Day Five:** 1. Answers will vary. 2. a. We are to submit to one another out of respect for Christ. This can make submitting easier because we are not doing it because the other person is better than us or because they deserve our respect. We do it because we respect Jesus. b. The reward for honoring parents is a long life. c. Answers will vary. d. God wants you to do your jobs as if you are working for Him. He wants you to work wholeheartedly. 3. Answers will vary. 4. Memory verse. **Meaningful Makeover:** Answers will vary.

Week Three: Day One: 1. Answers will vary. 2. Answers will vary. 3. a. Jesus tells us not to worry about what we will eat or drink, our body, our clothes, or about how long we will live. b. Answers will vary but might include something like: We worry about having the "right" clothes. We worry if we're pretty enough or thin enough. We might become obsessive about what we eat or drink. c. Answers will vary, but a possible answer would be: Seeking God's kingdom means not being so concerned about all the stuff in the world, and thinking more about what is eternal. d. Verse 34 tells us to live one day at a time; don't fret needlessly about things that may never happen or be consumed by worry over things we cannot control. 4. Answers will vary. 5. Memory verse. **Day Two:** 1. Answers will vary. 2. a. God is our refuge—He gives us protection (v. 1). God gives us every good thing (v. 2: "I have no good apart from you"). God gives us "counsel," or instruction (v. 7). God gives us security (v. 8: "I shall not be shaken"). God gives us gladness (v. 9). God gives us joy and eternal pleasures (v. 11). b. Answers will vary. c. Answers will vary. 3. Answers will vary. 4. Memory verse. **Day Three:** 1. Answers will vary. 2. Answers will vary. 3. a. God hears our voice. We can expect Him to answer. b. God will answer when we call on Him. c. The Lord hears our cry for mercy. We can trust Him to help us. d. The Lord hears us when we cry out. He saves us from our troubles. He is close to those who are brokenhearted. 4. Answers will vary. 5. Memory verse. **Day Four:** 1. Answers will vary. 2. Answers will vary. 3. a. We can give God thanks because He can change our mourning into dancing—our sadness into joy. b. We can give God thanks because He is near us, and we remember the things He has done for us in the past. c. We can give God thanks because He is good to us and will always love us. 4. Answers will vary. 5. Memory verse. **Study Styles:** Answers will vary but can include: Promise: "And the peace of God, which surpasses all understanding, will guard your hearts and your minds in Christ Jesus" (v. 7). Example: In verse 9, Paul tells the Philippians to follow his example. Attitude: Be joyful (v. 4). Command: "Do not be anxious about anything" (v. 6). Enlargement: "The God of peace will be with you" (v. 9). God is with us. **Day Five:** 1. Answers will vary. 2. a. David asks God to search him and know his heart and thoughts. b. Answers will vary but might include: fear over knowing God is aware of some sinful thoughts, comfort that God knows us so well, peace that we can be totally honest with God and He will still love us. 3. Answers will vary. 4. Memory verse. **Meaningful Makeover:** Answers will vary.

Week Four: Day One: 1. Answers will vary. 2. Answers will vary. 3. a. One possible definition: not arrogant or assertive. b. Answers will vary. One possible answer: A humble person doesn't think she is better than other people, doesn't have to be right all the time, and is willing to serve others. c. One specific way younger people can show humility is to accept the authority of older people. d. If we humble ourselves, God promises to lift us up in honor—exalt us—at the right time. 4. Answers will vary. 5. Memory verse. **Day Two:** 1. Answers will vary. 2. Answers will vary, but possible answers are: a. Pride is focusing on yourself. B. Humility is thinking more about others. 3. a. With pride comes disgrace. b. Pride will bring a person down. c. The proud and the haughty will be brought low. 4. Answers will vary. 5. Memory verse. **Day Three:** 1. Answers will vary. 2. Answers will vary. 3. a. Consider others more important than ourselves. Be interested in others. b. He took the form of a servant. He was born in the likeness of men. He became obedient to the point of death. He didn't hang onto equality with God. c. Answers will vary. 4. Answers will vary. 5. Memory verse. **Day Four:** 1. Answers will vary. 2. Answers will vary. 3. Answers will vary. 4. Answers will vary. 5. Memory verse. **Study Styles:** Possible answers using verses listed: 2 Chronicles 7:14: If we humble ourselves and repent, God will hear us and forgive our sins. Psalm 25:9: God leads and teaches those who are humble. Psalm 149:4: The Lord adorns the humble with salvation. Daniel 4:37: God is able to humble those who are proud. James 4:10: Humble yourself before the Lord and He will lift you up. **Day Five:** 1. Answers will vary. 2. a. God noticed her humility. b. Possible answer: Humility was important because she would certainly be ridiculed for being pregnant before she was married. Life would not be easy. She had to be willing to be a servant of God. c. Possible answer: I don't think she is bragging. She says people will call her blessed because *God* has done great things, not because *she* has done great things. d. He gives mercy to those who fear Him. He scatters the proud. He brings down the mighty. He exalts the humble. He fills the hungry with good things. e. Answers will vary. 3. Answers will vary. 4. Memory verse. **Meaningful Makeover:** Answers will vary.

Week Five: Day One: 1. Answers will vary. 2. Answers will vary. 3. a. Envy leads to evil. b. Envy "rots the bones"—it affects the health of the body. c. Envy and jealousy can lead to disorder and evil practices. 4. Answers will vary. 5. Memory verse. **Day Two:** 1. Answers will vary. 2. Answers will vary. 3. a. Asaph was envious of the wealth, health, and freedom from trouble others seemed to have. b. Answers will vary. c. Asaph went into God's sanctuary—into God's presence—and discerned their end. c. Possible answer: When we are in God's presence, we realize that most other things don't matter. We feel God's love and grace. 4. Answers will vary. 5. Memory verse. **Day Three:** 1. Answers will vary. 2. a. Leah felt she was hated. She didn't feel her husband loved her. Rachel envied Leah because Leah had children. b. Envy affected their relationship with each other, as it made the sisters fight. Envy affected their relationship with Jacob, as Rachel became angry with Jacob and blamed him for not giving her children—and then she inserted her maid into their marriage relationship as a "surrogate"! Also, Jacob's "anger was kindled" against Rachel. c. Answers will vary. 3. Answers will vary. 4. Memory verse. **Day Four:** 1. a. Possible answer: To be content is to be satisfied with what one is or has, not wanting more or anything else. b. Contentment is trusting God's care of me. c. Answers will vary. 2. Paul's secret for contentment was finding his strength in God. 3. Answers will vary. 4. Memory verse. **Study Styles:** Possible answers for up arrow: Verse 3: God heals my soul and leads me. Verse 4: God is with me; He comforts me. Verse 5: God gives me many blessings. Possible answers for down arrow: Verse 4: I don't have to be afraid because God is with me. Verse 6: I will be with God in heaven forever. Other markings will vary. **Day Five:** 1. Answers will vary. 2. a. The sacrifice of thanksgiving glorifies God. b. Thanksgiving can be a sacrifice because sometimes life is hard and it's difficult to find something to be thankful about. c. Answers will vary. d. Answers will vary. 3. Answers will vary. 4. Memory verse. **Meaningful Makeover:** Answers will vary.

Week Six: Day One: 1. Answers will vary. 2. Answers will vary. 3. a. The psalmist prays that God will turn his heart away from selfishness. b. We are not to act out of selfish ambition, but out of humility. 4. a. It is more blessed to give than to receive. The Greek word for *blessed* can also mean "happy," so the Bible is telling us that, ultimately, giving will make us happier than getting. b. We should not give because we have to, but because we want to. God loves a cheerful giver. 5. Answers will vary. 6. Memory verse. **Day Two:** 1. Answers will vary. 2. a. The young man called Jesus "Good Teacher." b. I think it showed that he didn't really view Jesus as God, but simply as a wise man. c. The young man wanted eternal life. d. Answers will vary but might include recognizing the fact that our stuff is not eternal; we can't take it to heaven with us. 3. Answers will vary. 4. Memory verse. **Day Three:** 1. Answers will vary. 2. a. ii. please God. b. iv. stay away from sexual immorality. c. iii. God. 3. Answers will vary but might include dressing modestly, choosing movies and books that don't portray sex before marriage, choosing friends who will support a choice of purity. 4. Answers will vary. 5. Memory verse. **Day Four:** 1. Answers will vary. 2. a. Answers will vary but might include the idea that laying down our lives might mean laying down our preferences and letting others have their way; laying down our comfort and serving when it's hard; or laying down our money and giving, even when we'd rather buy something for ourselves. b. We can show God's love is inside us by giving to people in need. c. Answers will vary. 3. Answers will vary. 4. Memory verse. **Study Styles:** Answers will vary; possible answers for the sample questions might include: **What?** The theme is love and service to others. **Where?** True change comes in our minds being made new. **Who?** We should love one another. **When?** We should be patient when we are experiencing tough times. **Why?** We serve one another because we are all members of the Body of Christ. **How?** We can serve unselfishly by using our gifts: speaking about God, serving others, teaching, encouraging others, giving to those in need, leading when called upon, and showing kindness. **Day Five:** 1. Answers will vary. 2. a. Answers will vary. b. The Bible says he wanted to "justify himself." Maybe he thought he was doing a good job of loving the people who lived in his neighborhood. c. The Greek root word of *neighbor* means "nearby, close." "Therefore it means 'whoever happens to be nearby or close at hand,' not just people who have homes nearby."[21] Jesus was making the point that a neighbor is anyone who needs our help. 3. Answers will vary. 4. Memory verse. **Meaningful Makeover:** Answers will vary.

Week Seven: Day One: 1. Answers will vary. 2. Answers are the Bible verses and personal evaluations. 3. Answers will vary. 4. Answers will vary. 5. Memory verse. **Day Two:** 1. Answers will vary. 2. Answers will vary. 3. a. A friend hurt David, broke a promise, and taunted him. b. Answers will vary. c. Verses 16–17: The Lord will hear our prayers. Verse 18: The Lord keeps us safe. Verse 22: The Lord will carry our burdens and give us strength. Verse 23: The Lord will defeat our enemies. d. Answers will vary. 4. Answers will vary. 5. Memory verse. **Day Three:** 1. Answers will vary. 2. a. His brothers had sold him into slavery, but now he was a powerful ruler who could use his power to get revenge. b. Joseph told them not to be distressed or angry. Joseph saw God's purpose in all that had happened. c. Joseph saw that God had sent him to Egypt to save lives, including the lives of his own family. d. Answers will vary. 3. Answers will vary. 4. Memory verse. **Day Four:** 1. Answers will vary. 2. a. Two important parts of prayer are 1) believing God answers prayer and 2) forgiving anyone against whom you are holding a grudge. b. Unforgiveness blocks our relationship with God. If we don't forgive others, God does not forgive us. 3. Answers will vary. 4. Memory verse. **Study Styles:** Possible answers: Compassionate: sympathetic, kind, considerate. Kindness: tenderness, sweetness, helpfulness, goodness. Humility: not thinking too highly of oneself, meekness. Meekness: patience, being unassuming. Patience: willingness to endure, self-control, serenity. Bear: to tolerate, support, hold up. Forgive: excuse, let it go, pardon. **Day Five:** 1. Answers will vary. 2. Answers will vary. 3. a. Don't tell secrets; betrayal will separate friends. b. Forgiveness shows love. Constantly bringing up past mistakes will break up friendships. c. A wise person knows when not to speak and keeps her cool. 4. Answers will vary. 5. Memory verse. **Meaningful Makeover:** Answers will vary.

Week Eight: Day One: 1. Answers will vary. 2. Answers will vary. 3. Answers will vary. 4. a. The psalm realizes the beautiful creation of the human body and praises God for His marvelous work. b. Answers will vary. c. Answers will vary. 5. Answers will vary. 6. Memory verse. **Day Two:** 1. Answers will vary. 2. 1 Kings 8:61: A beautiful heart is completely true to the Lord. Mark 11:23: A beautiful heart doesn't doubt, but believes. Romans 5:5: A beautiful heart is full of love given by the Holy Spirit. Galatians 4:6: A beautiful heart has God's

Spirit. 3. Answers will vary. 4. Memory verse. **Day Three:** 1. Answers will vary. 2. b. Jesus was humble. c. Jesus was a servant. d. Jesus was forgiving. 3. Answers will vary. 4. Memory verse. **Day Four:** 1. Answers will vary. 2. Answers will vary. 3. Answers will vary. 4. Memory verse. **Study Styles:** Answers will vary. Examples of possible answers would be: Step 2: Character Quality—bravery; Step 3: How Esther Demonstrated That Quality—She went to the king even though it might have meant her death; Step 4: A Verse That Shows That Quality—Esther 4:16; Step 5: How I Will Apply It to My Life This Week—I will do the right thing, even if it means I won't be liked by my peers. **Day Five:** 1. Answers will vary. 2. Answers will vary. 3. Answers will vary. 4. Memory verse. **Meaningful Makeover:** Answers will vary.

★★★★★★★

Endnotes

1. www.huffingtonpost.com/2012/05/02/julia-bluhm-protest-airbrushing-seventeen-magazine_n_1471876.html, July 19, 2013.

2. http://www.keirsey.com/4temps/fieldmarshal.asp, July 31, 2013.

3. http://www.qideas.org/video/the-evolution-of-the-swimsuit.aspx, June 27, 2013.

4. http://www.tumblr.com/tagged/jason%20evert, June 27, 2013.

5. http://www.theglobeandmail.com/news/national/education/toronto-school-study-paints-a-picture-of-teens-under-pressure/article8485352/, June 26, 2013.

6. http://forum.purseblog.com/handbags-and-purses/must-read-stats-facts-quirky-quotes-about-almighty-37517.html, August 22, 2013.

7. http://www.gratitudepower.net/science.htm, August 22, 2013.

8. http://abcnews.go.com/Business/prom-costs-rise-percent-national-average-1139/story?id=19051387#.UeBKz21t4-c, July 12, 2013.

9. http://www.thefreedictionary.com/Pride, July 11, 2013.

10. Ibid.

11. Ibid.

12. http://www.mentalhelp.net/poc/view_doc.php?type=doc&id=28588&cn=0, July 31, 2013.

13. Based on statistics from *State of the Media: The Social Media Report 2012.* http://www.nielsen.com/content/dam/corporate/us/en/reports-downloads/2012-Reports/The-Social-Media-Report-2012.pdf, July 24, 2013.

14. http://www.brainyquote.com/quotes/quotes/h/haroldcoff106198.html, August 9, 2013.

15. http://www.gratitudepower.net/science.htm, July 31, 2013.

16. http://living.msn.com/style-beauty/simply-chic-blog-post/?post=305ed493-2f1b-48f1-8f8e-1d9cd5f6e90a, August 22, 2013.

17. http://www.whatchristianswanttoknow.com/20-amazing-quotes-about-serving, August 16, 2013.

18. http://www.brainyquote.com/quotes/quotes/l/lewisbsme135524.html, August 9, 2013.

19. http://www.nytimes.com2008/09/11/fashion/11talk.html?pagewanted=all&_r=0, August 3, 2013.

20. Copyright James Werning, "Mirror" (www.peacedude.net). Used by permission. All rights reserved.

21. *The Lutheran Study Bible* (St. Louis, MO: Concordia Publishing House, 2009), 1735, note on Luke 10:29. Used by permission. All rights reserved.

Images/Art Credits